STITCHED FROM THE SOUL

A turn-of-the-century photograph of my paternal grandmother, Pleasant Ann ("P.A.") Fry, an elementary-school teacher and skilled seamstress. Few people in the town of Bastrop, Texas, my father's place of birth, knew her first name; she preferred to be addressed by her initials in order to avoid a first-name familiarity. My interest in slave-made quilts began when I was quite young, as I listened to my father tell stories about his great-grandmother, Amanda, a slave in southeastern Arkansas. Amanda had been described to him with great pride by "P.A." as a plantation "sewing woman." Although none of her handiwork has survived, accounts of Amanda's considerable creativity and artistic skills remain a large and fascinating part of my family's oral tradition, and were the spark that initiated this book.

STITCHED FROM THE SOUL
Slave Quilts from the Ante-Bellum South

Gladys-Marie Fry, Ph.D.

DUTTON STUDIO BOOKS

Dutton Studio Books   New York

In association with the
Museum of American Folk Art   New York

DUTTON STUDIO BOOKS

Published by the Penguin Group
Penguin Books USA Inc., 375 Hudson Street,
New York, New York, 10014, U.S.A.

Penguin Books Ltd, 27 Wrights Lane,
London W8 5TZ, England

Penguin Books Australia Ltd, Ringwood,
Victoria, Australia

Penguin Books Canada Ltd, 2801 John Street,
Markham, Ontario, Canada L3R 1B4

Penguin Books (N.Z.) Ltd, 182–190 Wairau Road,
Auckland 10, New Zealand

Penguin Books Ltd, Registered Offices:
Harmondsworth, Middlesex, England

First published by Dutton Studio Books, an imprint of Penguin Books USA Inc.

First printing, November, 1990
10   9   8   7   6   5   4   3   2

Library of Congress
Catalog Card Number: 89-50829

Printed and bound by Dai Nippon Printing Co., Ltd., Tokyo, Japan
Book designed by Nancy Danahy

ISBN: 0-525-24842-0 (cloth); ISBN: 0-525-48535-X (DP)

To my *father*, Louis Edwin Fry, Sr., keeper of the family stories concerning his slave great-grandmother, Amanda, seamstress and quilter on an Arkansas plantation; to my *mother*, Obelia Swearingen Fry, who wanted to travel to see each historical quilt that turned up on my twelve-year search; and to my *brother*, Louis Edwin Fry, Jr., who, early on, felt that this project was worth doing, and kept prodding me—gently and sometimes not so gently—to complete this task.

ACKNOWLEDGMENTS

Any project that has surveyed fifteen states and one country overseas (England) has to involve networking on many levels. First, a general thank-you to all of the people who responded to my query letters and telephone calls.

I would also like to acknowledge three former mentors, now deceased: Dr. Williston H. Lofton and Rayford W. Logan, professors emeritus in history, Howard University, who first aroused my interest in slave history; and Dr. Richard H. Dorson, Distinguished Professor, Folklore Institute, Indiana University, who encouraged me to pursue the study of oral and material forms of slave culture.

The historians and art historians who helped shape this study from its beginning in terms of concept and direction are Dr. Robert Farris Thompson and Dr. John Blassingame of Yale University; Dr. Ira Berlin, University of Maryland; and Dr. Jacqueline A. Groggin, Manuscript Division, Library of Congress.

A number of museums provided helpful information, photographs, and so forth. A few museums and their staffs extended help on more than one occasion. Of these, I would specifically like to thank Doris Bowman, Division of Textiles, Smithsonian Institution; Dr. Harry Robinson, African-American Museum, Dallas, Texas; Mattye Reed, founder of the Heritage Center, North Carolina Agricultural and Technical University, Greensboro, North Carolina; Dr. George McDaniel, Atlanta Historical Society; Joey Brackman, Alabama Council for the Arts; Cecilia Steinfelt, San Antonio Museum Association; Laurel Horton, McKissick Museum, Columbia, South Carolina; and Carolyn J. Weekley, Curator, the Abby Aldrich Rockefeller Folk Art Center of the Colonial Williamsburg Foundation.

Four librarians from McKeldin Library, University of Maryland, deserve to be acknowledged for assisting with various phases of this project. They are Judith Cmero, Head, Interlibrary Loan; Dolores Huff, Lending Supervisor, Interlibrary Loan; Jean Kish, Reference; and Jim Kelly, Cataloging.

Several of my colleagues at the University of Maryland turned into academic sleuths as they combed flea markets, antiques shows, and libraries in an effort to find slave artifacts and the documentation concerning them. They are Dr. Lewis Lawson, Dr. Virginia Beauchamp, Dr. Margaret Ordonez, Betty Fern, and Cathy Jung.

Staff in the English department at the University of Maryland—Terri Hrudz and Molly Brennan—assisted in processing the data, transcribing nineteenth-century letters, typing, and so forth. Dr. Leigh Ryan assisted in every phase of the project. Her help was essential in completing this manuscript.

My friends helped in ways too numerous to mention. They are Jacqueline Troup Bobo, Michael Owen Jones, Bettye Ward, Cynthia Elyce Rubin, Nancy Fitch, Ricky Clarke, Eleanor Alexander, Joan Perkal, Dr. Jessie Carney Smith, Dr. Mary Arnold Twining, Jamie Darr, Rachel Ripple, Gail Hansberry, Viola Leak, Essie Leak, Mary Margaret Camus, and John C. Richardson. Two friends—Dr. Stanley Warren and Aletha Hendrickson—went the proverbial last mile in assisting with this project. I owe them a great deal for all their efforts on my behalf. A special thank-you to Judy Taggart, my friend and editor, and JT&A, who helped me to meet my deadline. A generous thank-you to all of the individuals who allowed me to photograph their family quilts for this collection.

Finally, a special thank-you to my father, Professor Louis Edwin Fry, Sr., who made manuscript suggestions and helped select the photographs for the slave cabins that are used in this book. In the 1930s, my father surveyed surviving slave cabins in central Alabama with the assistance of a grant from the Phelps Stokes Fund.

Funding for this book was supported in part by a grant from the National Endowment for the Humanities. In addition, part of the research for this study was conducted while I held a fellowship awarded by the Smithsonian Institution. Additional monies were provided in the form of faculty research support awards from the University of Maryland. I would especially like to thank Dr. James Lesher, Acting Dean for Arts and Humanities of the University of Maryland, for his support and encouragement of this project.

CONTENTS

FOREWORD

When, in 1982, I first discussed with Dr. Gladys-Marie Fry the possibility of a research project leading to an exhibition and book, little did either of us realize the complexity of what I was suggesting. The exhibit, "Stitched from the Soul: Slave Quilts from the Ante-Bellum South," mounted at the newly opened Eva and Morris Feld Branch of the Museum of American Folk Art, New York City, in the summer of 1989; the accompanying symposium organized by Egle Zygas, the Museum of American Folk Art Curator of Education; and this book, published by Dutton Studio Books in association with the Museum, must all be viewed as work-in-progress.

Gladys-Marie Fry, a well-known scholar and Professor of Folklore at the University of Maryland, College Park, has provided through her many major research efforts new insights into the lives and creativity of slave women in America during the eighteenth and nineteenth centuries. To illustrate her valuable text, she undertook a national search to discover textiles that would visually augment her discoveries in such primary documents as diaries, family records, plantation records, and account books. When possible, she went to inspect personally bedcovers that had passed down through several generations and were believed to have been slave made.

Anyone who has pursued this method of research knows that pitfalls can and will develop. Traditions rooted in family history are frequently incorrect. Myths and personal associations to known quiltmakers and coverlet weavers disappeared in the light of the author's ongoing investigation and study.

Because of the pioneering nature of this project the Museum felt it was prudent to seek advice from quilt scholars and the opinions of textile conservationists regarding the bedcovers being considered for the exhibit. Several quilts were eliminated because the fabrics used were simply not available in the period under investigation, and others were rejected because it was felt that they were too fragile to be exhibited, even in the carefully protected Museum setting. And, finally, Dr. Fry convinced the Museum staff that scholarship would be served by including pieces that were created by makers who had found new ideas of design once they had been freed from bondage.

In all of this there were certain risks—risks that to us at the Museum seemed worth taking. For it is only with projects of this sort that new information and new knowledge develop.

The completion of "Stitched from the Soul: Slave Quilts from the Ante-Bellum South"—a major research project in a new field of investigation—has provided many ideas for consideration. Ongoing scholarship will undoubtedly challenge and enrich this first exhibition and book.

It is our hope that others will both pursue and expand our efforts. As additional and possibly revisionist ideas develop and are confirmed, they will be reported through *The Clarion*, America's Folk Art Magazine, and through The Quilt Connection newsletter, a special publication for quilt enthusiasts recently developed by the Museum of American Folk Art.

DR. ROBERT BISHOP
Director

PREFACE

Many of the various roles and contributions of slave women to plantation life have been swept under the rug of history. While slave men have long been acknowledged as skilled carpenters, brick masons, iron makers, furniture makers, wood-carvers, and potters, women have been seen primarily in the role of the plantation "mammy" figure. This limited view of slave women has made them the victim of three *isms*: racism, sexism, and regionalism.

In particular, the contribution of slave women to textile production and other craft processes has been ignored. Yet the evidence that slave women produced fabric, and that they quilted, sewed, and crocheted is irrefutable. A significant number of slave-made quilts is now preserved in fifteen states and England. As for other textiles, many woven coverlets, counterpanes, rag rugs, bed rugs, and crocheted artifacts attributed to the handiwork of slave women have been located.

Even today, a slave-made quilting frame in Arlington, Virginia, is still being used daily by a handful of elderly African-American women at a senior citizens center. At their daily meeting, these women quilt, talk, laugh, and gossip—a few have even been known to smoke a pipe!

To date, no formal study has been undertaken to determine the extent of the involvement of slave women in the design or craftsmanship of mid-nineteenth-century quilts, or to determine the influence of African culture on African-American quilting styles. Thus, for too long have slave women been denied recognition or acknowledgment—or even a history.

That history, however, has been inscribed in the quilts that survive. Many record family history and legends, as they express the personal philosophy and religious beliefs of their makers. The efforts of these slaves in making artifacts both beautiful and useful remain unexcelled in design and craftsmanship.

Quilting also provided an outlet for slaves—a means of developing hidden talents and establishing a kind of emotional stability and independence. Quilting offered time for introspection and reflection, and a means of gaining perspective and control. Denied the opportunity to record their thoughts on paper, slaves unconsciously left careful records of their emotional and psychological well-being on each surviving quilt. Clues are to be found, for example, in the consistency of the stitching pattern; the relative length and evenness reflect a certain amount of inner harmony. Deviations from this pattern might well indicate that the quilt maker was nursing physical and emotional wounds. Color preferences and abrupt changes in design might also serve as indicators of general well-being.

Additional physical clues might be stains from tears or blood. All of these clues help us trace the life cycles of individual slave women, as well as chart their experiences and the knowledge they gained along the way.

In a sense, the stitches, the tears, and the blood are "time markers" of the everyday events in their lives: marriages, births of children, illnesses, separation of family members by sale or death, whippings, punishment, deprivation, and so forth.

Denied the opportunity to read or write, slave women quilted their diaries, creating permanent but unwritten records of events large and small, of pain and loss, of triumph and tragedy in their lives. And each piece of cloth became the focal point of a remembered past.

African-American quilts have remained an untapped source of cultural study, but perhaps the American consciousness is being awakened. Jesse Jackson's fiery speech to the Democratic Convention in Atlanta, Georgia, on July 19, 1988, referred to the quilting tradition in his family:

> When I was a child growing up in Greenville, South Carolina, and Grandmomma could not afford a blanket, she didn't complain, and we did not freeze. Instead, she took pieces of old cloth—patches—wool, silk, gaberdeen [sic], crockersack—only patches, barely good enough to wipe off your shoes with. But they didn't stay that way very long. With sturdy hands and a strong cord, she sewed them together into a quilt, a thing of beauty and power and culture. (*The New York Times*, July 21, 1988)

Great-grandmother Fannie Kelly, my mother's grandmother, managed to keep her eleven grandchildren warm during many rigorous Missouri winters by making similar quilts. My mother told me:

And I remember that Grandma Kelly would make these quilts out of large blocks or squares. She used any kind of material that was available. Any cloth that had outgrown its usefulness in one form, such as a dress or overalls, was given new life in her quilts. Sometimes these quilts were double-sided; she had one design on one side and another on the reverse. And I can tell you one thing. When we got into bed with one of Grandma's quilts, we chose our sleeping positions carefully, because once the quilt was pulled up over your body, you couldn't *move* for the rest of the night. It didn't matter what you wanted to get up and do—you just couldn't move!

My dad's reminiscences are similar. His mother, a school teacher in Bastrop, Texas, and a skilled seamstress, made all of the family's quilts during her summer hiatus from teaching. My dad considered them physically a part of the household furnishings. In fact, he remembers using one of these quilts on a premarital picnic with my mother, rather than run the risk of getting grass stains on his "store-bought" blanket. My dad explains, "Obviously, I wouldn't do this now. But in those days—the 1920s—I thought of it just as an old quilt Mama had made."

A common thread bonds Jesse Jackson's grandmother with my own, as well as with the slave women who preceded them. They all assembled their quilts of memory patches—bits and pieces of private, personal history indelibly etched in their minds: the worn-out work dress, Grandpa's old vest, the bandanna that came as a gift one Christmas morning. These memories linked them to a remembered African past, and served as a point of contact with generations yet unborn.

GLADYS-MARIE FRY

College Park, Maryland
Spring 1990

PROLOGUE

The process of constructing an actual quilt provides a metaphor for my work in putting together this monograph on slave-made quilts. I began with the idea that perhaps enough slave-made quilts and other artifacts existed to tell a story, and then, scrap by scrap, collected historical data and artifacts finally to piece together a finished product that sheds new light on the meaning of quilts in the lives of slave men and women. Several stages have been involved in this process.

Methodology

In 1976, I researched and wrote a monograph on the life of Harriet Powers, a remarkable quilter and former slave from Athens, Georgia. Two of her quilts have survived, both concerning biblical subject matter and both now housed in major museums. Although she could neither read nor write, Powers recorded historical events with amazing accuracy in her quilts.

In 1979, I embarked on an ambitious plan to research and write a book on African-American quilting styles. I mailed thousands of letters to museums, private collectors, quilt shops, and scholars, asking for the names of African-American quilters in their communities. The stamped self-addressed envelopes I enclosed began to pay off as replies began drifting back to me.

Many people reported they had no information. But letters also began to trickle in with notes that essentially said, "I don't know any African-American women in my community who are currently quilting, but our historical society has quilts made by slaves. Are you interested in knowing more about that?"

The letters reminded me of the stories that my dad had told about his great-grandmother Amanda, a slave on an Arkansas plantation. According to our family stories, Amanda was a seamstress who could not only make almost any kind of textile—quilts, woven coverlets, rag rugs, exquisite embroidered or crocheted items—but could also do woodworking and ironworking. She was well known around her Arkansas plantation for being able to make almost anything out of any material.

As the trickle of letters turned into a small stream, I became incredulous. It was 1979, 114 years after the end of the Civil War, and I was discovering more and more surviving slave quilts. I realized that perhaps I could focus on this aspect of my interest in African-American quilts.

I believe that the quilts I have located thus far represent the proverbial tip of the iceberg. Undoubtedly, many surviving slave-made quilts remain in the hands of both African-American and white families who have retained them over several generations. But locating these families can be difficult. The lecture circuit has been a useful research tool, with the ensuing question-and-answer period often producing a helpful exchange of information. A lecture at the Bethune Museum and Archives in Washington, D.C., for example, resulted in my locating thirteen quilts made by the same slave quilter. Similar leads developed from other lectures given throughout the country between 1983 and 1987. Networking also played a significant role in my search. Friends asked friends; others poked through flea markets and covered major antiques shows.

The problem was not only to locate the artifacts themselves (the quilts, quilting frames, sewing houses, and so forth), but to locate corroborating written data concerning the slave-made quilts.

The Problem of Researching the History of Slave Women

Researching the quilting traditions of African-American women has been hampered by two major problems: the scarcity of data concerning slave women in written historical sources; and the task of documenting slave-made quilts.

To research slave women's quilting history, I have relied on the following types of sources: (1) official historical accounts; (2) the testimony of former slaves from the WPA Federal Writers Project and other nineteenth-century writings by African Americans; and (3) oral tradition, primarily family accounts pertaining to the provenance of their own surviving slave-made quilts. Each type of source has its own strengths and weaknesses.

To offset the weaknesses, I made an effort to corroborate information obtained from each source by weighing internal evidence and confirming it against the other sources of information.

Because of major gaps in their historiography,

1. Photograph of a former slave, "Mammy Sally," who was a house servant on an ante-bellum plantation. (Manuscript Department, University of Virginia Library, Charlottesville, Virginia)

slave women were included less often than men in eighteenth- and nineteenth-century historical accounts. This point is clearly evident in the computerized files of the Museum of Early Southern Decorative Arts in Winston-Salem, North Carolina.

Only two women are found among the twenty-five hundred pre-1822 slave artisans recorded by the museum. Trades range from the more common carpenter, wheelwright, shipwright, and bricklayer to the less common coppersmith, bookbinder, gunsmith, and upholsterer. Only eight weavers or weaver apprentices and two dyers are listed, and here are found the only women on the list—Hester Hyeth, a free African-American artisan and carpet weaver, and Kim (who may be male), a slave artisan and weaver. Nowhere is there any reference to typically female trades, like that of seamstress.

A variety of reasons may explain this phenomenon: the general status of women in the antebellum South and the perceived value of their work, and the fact that much handicraft was probably done in "spare" time and was not considered a main "trade."

In my search for more information, I extensively examined the following types of official historical accounts:
• Southern travel accounts
• Plantation records maintained by women
• Autobiographies of Southern planters
• Memoirs, reminiscences, and diaries.
All of these historical sources have yielded surprisingly little material about quilting. In fact, Dr. John Blassingame, a history professor at Yale, suggested to me that trying to find data about slave quilting in general historical sources was like trying to find a "needle in a haystack." This lack of references in white sources was also supported in a letter (April 22, 1985) from Eugene Genovese, author of *Roll, Jordan, Roll*:

> ...Apparently, so far as the white folks were concerned, those quilts were products of their own lily hands or did not exist. Not a word [in reading of plantation manuscripts and family letters]. No mention of slaves at quilting bees at all. It will, I am sure, come as no surprise to you that, in certain respects, black people did not exist while they were nonetheless ever-present and ever-discussed.

This problem of historical omission reached into all written materials. Official public records, such as those noting births, deaths, and wills, tended almost totally to exclude nineteenth-century African-Americans. Plantation records, except for larger plantations, tended to be either nonexistent or incomplete. Planters who wrote at all were interested in describing plantation life as it pertained to their official duties. What the slaves did on their own time, if it was not illegal, was of little interest to them.

But other aspects, too, influenced what planters omitted from their writings. Except for quilting bees, the solitary act of quilting would have been witnessed only by family members, and many plantation owners might have known little, if anything, about it. As "women's work," quilting would also have been considered unimportant.

2. Daguerreotype of Isaac Jefferson, a slave from Petersburg, Virginia, c. 1845. (Manuscript Department, University of Virginia Library, Charlottesville, Virginia)

3. Daguerreotype of a skilled slave nurse, c. 1850. (Manuscript Department, University of Virginia Library, Charlottesville, Virginia)

3. Slave quilt makers used an inferior grade cotton (not top quality).
4. Slave-made quilts always had a backing that was "make-do."
5. Certain evidence of a slave-made quilt was that cotton seeds could be found in the lining.

An example of this bias is the perpetuation of the notion that slave women either picked the cotton used in antebellum quilts or simply "assisted" the plantation mistress in quilting projects. Another frequently reported notion was the fact that slaves added to the plantation mistress's responsibilities.

Such a view is stated by Michael Berry in the February/March 1985 issue of *American Craft*: "Some slave-made quilts have survived, but they are extremely difficult to document because of the social structure under which the slave lived. For the most part, however, sewing chores, from fancywork to mending, fell to the mistress of the household."

One of the most persistent myths concerning the African-American heritage in the United States is that quilt making by slaves was not an important tradition. This myth is based on the argument that African-American women (and men, in a few instances) were too busy working in the fields all day to have time to quilt. Inherent in this argument is the belief that

Omission has extended also to specialized quilting histories, journals, and periodicals. Before 1960, African-American women were rarely mentioned. After 1960, the one quilter most frequently mentioned was Harriet Powers.

General historical accounts of nineteenth-century African-Americans, until recently, focused on the economic and political aspects of the system. Data that dealt with African-American slave culture, either oral or material, were virtually excluded, except in some accounts written by Northern or foreign visitors. Looking at slave life from the outside, they were more interested in all of its aspects. Certainly, historical accounts contained little mention of African survivals among African-American slaves.

But authenticity of historical records, usually scanty at best, is only one problem. Bias is another. Southern white stereotyped thinking regarding the artistic worth of slave-made quilts manifests itself in the following myths:

1. Any crudely made pre–Civil War quilt could be identified as a slave-made quilt.
2. Any pre–Civil War quilt with large, uneven stitches was made by a slave.

4. Ambrotype of an unidentified male slave. (The Valentine Museum, Richmond, Virginia)

African-Americans in America lacked sufficient artistic talent to create aesthetically satisfying artifacts.

A second, and perhaps even more damaging, stereotype is the notion that the quilts made by slave women on antebellum plantations were crafted under the watchful eye of the mistress and were made according to nineteenth-century concepts of Euro-American design traditions. In other words, individual creativity and improvisation are thought to have been nonexistent.

In fact, slave quilters, who were forced by plantation rules to work within a Euro-American tradition, found inventive ways to disguise within the quilt improvisational forms and elements from African cosmology and mythology. A strong and continued belief in cosmology is evidenced by representations of the sun, the Congo cross, and the frequent use of red and white, which comes from the Shango cult of Nigeria.

The influence of African mythology survived in the snake motif, which is a symbol of Damballah, the West African god of fertility. Symbols of Erzulie, the Vodun goddess of love, appeared in slave-made textiles in the form of intricate flower patterns.

As evidence of these myths concerning slave-made quilts and other handcrafted artifacts, I offer the following excerpt from a letter I received from the president of a Southern historical society:

5. Ambrotype of an unidentified slave woman. (The Valentine Museum, Richmond, Virginia)

6. Whitewashed-brick slave cabins from The Hermitage, Chatham County, Georgia. (Historic American Building Survey, Photographic Collection, Library of Congress, Washington, D.C.)

7. Three surviving mid-nineteenth-century brick slave cabins from Virginia. (Virginia State Library)

Quilts made by slave labor in the South were a sorry affair, both as to the pattern devised and the workmanship thereof. Some few slaves were educated well enough to sew.... But all the clothing on the plantation—for white and black—was made by the wife of the plantation owner—working night and day.

Quilts made in that period of time were made with cotton batting, which, when washed (in a black pot with lye soap), lumped up, faded, and was ruined. They were usually filthy.

The best historical evidence for an active pre–Civil War quilting tradition among slaves was what they themselves told interviewers for the WPA Federal Writers Project and remembered in their own autobiographies. In both these sources, former slave women frequently mentioned quilting either for the plantation mistress or for themselves. A careful sifting of this material enabled me to learn about the role that making quilts played in the lives of slave women and the meaning quilting held for them. In other words, these two sources confirmed each other.

Documenting Slave-Made Textiles

It is irrelevant to say that documenting authentic slave-made textiles is a difficult task. "Fully documented" slave-made textiles can be defined as those in which the provenance can be traced directly to a slave quilt maker. I have accepted as evidence of origin written data connecting the quilt with its maker, such as museum accession information, diaries, family letters, and oral tradition. Early (pre–World War II) accession cards give detailed information about the white donor family for whom the slave made the textile.

Such details as family military honors, political achievements, civic awards, and land ownership are frequently described. The slave quilt maker, on the other hand, is often dismissed with a sentence or two in which the slave is described as an "old negress," "unknown slave," or "slave girl." When slave quilt makers are identified, the term "aunt" (or "uncle") precedes the name. I did not locate a single accession card in which the slave quilt maker is fully identified either physically or in terms of plantation duties, family ties, or artistic versatility.

A number of textiles in this book have survived in the families of the original maker. Where no written authentication existed, I interviewed family members to obtain the slave quilt maker's life history. Family reminiscences concerning surviving slave-made quilts were corroborated, where possible, by checking such things as historical probability and the authenticity of both fabric and dyes.

The majority of textiles in this book were made by slave labor. It can be assumed that many more textiles

8. A nineteenth-century log cabin, possibly from Savannah, Georgia. The cabin has a mud chimney at the left that extended above the roof when the cabin was first built. (Photographic Collection, Library of Congress, Washington, D.C.)

9. A mid-ninteenth-century log cabin with a mud chimney and mud chinking. (Cook Collection, The Valentine Museum, Richmond, Virginia)

10. Women and children near Thomasville, Georgia, c. 1890. Although this is a later photograph, it shows typical slave quarters and the type of pot that the slaves turned over to contain the sound of their secret parties and meetings. (Hargrett Rare Book and Manuscript Library, University of Georgia Libraries, Athens, Georgia)

were made with the assistance of slaves. Unfortunately, written documentation or oral tradition concerning the slave quilt makers that may have accompanied the original textiles either was lost or the truth deliberately suppressed. The Civil War was a major contributing factor in the loss of eighteenth- and nineteenth-century quilts and their histories.

The African-American Design Aesthetic

Both historical and contemporary African-American quilts are shaped by a design aesthetic that differs from traditional Euro-American forms. The key question is, what is this aesthetic, and how does it manifest itself in African-American quilts? In recent years art historians and quilters have made an effort to answer this question by searching for common elements in this body of quilts. According to Robert Horton, author of *Calico and Beyond: The Use of Patterned Fabric in Quilts* (p. 44), six major design characteristics are found in African-American quilts:

1. Vertical strip organization
2. Bold color
3. Large design elements
4. Asymmetry
5. Multiple patterning
6. Improvised rhythm.

This effort, though useful, is perhaps misleading. How do you categorize a large body of quilts made by African-American women that simply do not fit within any of these categories? Perhaps it could be more accurately said that African-American quilt styles are eclectic—ranging from quilts with strong African influences to those that almost completely merge with Euro-American design traditions.

Quilt researcher Laurel Horton, in an oral presentation titled "Perspectives on African-American Quilts" given at the Southern Quilt Symposium in Chattanooga, Tennessee, on March 22, 1988, commented on the African-American design aesthetic and the problems inherent in pigeonholing these quilts.

> One reason I think that whites, especially white quilt makers, feel the need to categorize black quilt makers as different is because whites have defined "good" quilt making as showing tiny stitches and exhibiting one's *control* over the medium by making exact repetitions of carefully constructed blocks. Many traditional black quilt makers consider making lots of tiny stitches to be a waste of time and doing the same block over and over as boring. There is more than one definition of what makes a "good" quilt.

11. Interior of an African-American cabin of the late nineteenth century. Note the handmade bed covering. (Cook Collection, The Valentine Museum, Richmond, Virginia)

At the same time, though, white quilt makers are reluctant to accept the quilts made by white quilt makers that are characterized by some of the same free-wheeling designs as those of blacks. Picture this scene: a white quilt maker walks into a room and sees a quilt that includes a variety of bright colors and textures and in which the pattern looks a little different in each block.

The construction is "utilitarian." The viewer is confused. She knows that if it was made by a black woman it is part of the African-American tradition and is considered a good quilt, but if it was made by a white woman it does not follow the rules of European-American tradition and is not considered a good quilt. If she doesn't have information about the quilt maker she is not sure if she should like the quilt.

My first encounter with a distinctly African-American quilting aesthetic occurred in the mid-1970s. A colleague from the University of Maryland and I were trying to locate African-American quilters for a Maryland state festival. Various inquiries led us to the University of Maryland, Eastern Shore, in Princess Anne, Maryland. Once on the campus, the overwhelming consensus of the people we queried about local African-American quilters led us to a female employee of the university. We were told repeatedly that her grandmother made "gorgeous," "stunningly beautiful" quilts. I began to salivate with anticipation.

We quickly located the employee, but found her extremely reluctant to arrange a meeting with her grandmother, who, she allowed, "did not meet strangers well." At this point, the granddaughter said, "I really wish you could see these quilts, however, because they are so beautiful."

A meeting was finally agreed upon, following a hasty

phone call to her grandmother, on the condition that the granddaughter accompany us to "smooth the way."

After only a short drive into the town of Princess Anne, we found the grandmother, true to her word, waiting for us at the door. We exchanged greetings. She appeared to be in her early seventies. Her quilts, a half dozen or so, were neatly piled on the sofa.

I remember standing in the middle of the living-room floor with my eyes transfixed on the most unusual quilts I had ever seen! All of them were original designs, primarily composed of randomly sized pieces of cloth—principally wools—cut in assorted shapes. The center section of one of these quilts was made up of a large portion of a plaid pleated skirt!

What startled me—and the reason the memory of this encounter is still so vivid—was the *total* departure from a Euro-American design concept.

I praised the grandmother for her unique quilts, took down the appropriate information concerning the quilt maker, and left.

My education concerning the African-American quilt aesthetic had just begun. A "window" opened that day, bringing with it a fresh new perspective that erased my preconceived ideas of how African-American quilts should look. Never again would I look at African-American quilts in quite the same way.

Two types of quilts have been investigated in this study:

1. *Appliqué quilts.* Many of the slave-made quilts I have presented in this book were done in appliqué. It is my hypothesis that the appliqué tradition that flourished in the American South was brought over by slaves from Benin (formerly known as Dahomey), West Africa. In the Benin tapestries, stories from oral tradition and history are illustrated with appliquéd figures. Animals are used to symbolize kings or central figures of proverbs or folktales. The influence of Benin appliqué tradition on the Bible quilts executed by Harriet Powers, an ex-slave from Benin, has been firmly established by scholars, particularly in her technique and animal symbolism. Another intriguing aspect of Harriet Powers's quilts is the merging of Christian religious symbols with the African cosmology of the Bakongo people. An interesting aspect of appliqué work made by slaves in America—in contrast to Euro-American appliqué—is that when placed on a grid, the design elements in slave-made appliqués often fall above or below the containing lines. More investigation is required.

2. *Patchwork quilts.* "Patch" quilts were made from hand-sewn pieces of cloth varying in size from tiny scraps to fairly large rectangles or squares. Although

12. Interior of a slave cabin showing the central fireplace that provided the only source of heat and means of cooking. The iron pot is of the type that slaves believed would muffle the sound of secret meetings if it was turned upside down. (Cook Collection, The Valentine Museum, Richmond, Virginia)

The Pride of the Family.
Copyright 1897 by Strohmeyer & Wyman.

13. This stereoptican photograph, titled "Pride of the Family," is a staged version of how whites perceived the interior of slave cabins would look. Note the flax wheel and the rag rug. (Photographic Collection, Library of Congress, Washington, D.C.)

evidence does not yet confirm this point, slaves may have added to their own quilts such elements as stripes of random length and width that "framed" the geometrical patterns. This style was influenced by strip weaving done by West African males. Surviving quilts confirm that both appliqué and patchwork quilts were definitely made by slave women, and both types bear a strong resemblance to Euro-American designs.

In this book I have made an effort to present the context or setting in which the antebellum textiles were made. To do this, photographs of actual slaves are included along with the interior and exterior of their cabins, the sewing houses or loom rooms, and a variety of textiles that were made by both slave men and women. I have also tried to provide the social context in which slave quilting thrived by discussing the evening quilting bees, plantation quilting parties, and slave folklore.

THE SLAVE SEAMSTRESS

I was sitting upstairs in Old Miss house quilting when de first Yankee army boat went to Vicksburg, Mississippi. Old Miss made me git right up and go git her children out of school and bring 'em right home.[1]

The official historical position concerning the role of slave seamstresses and quilters is one of almost total silence. An example of this omission occurs in a 1934 history thesis written by Paula Jones at Southern Methodist University titled *Slave Women in the Old South.* The author discusses field slaves, house servants, the market women of Charleston, South Carolina, and the ubiquitous "mammy" figure. There is no mention, however, of skilled slave women in general, or slave seamstresses in particular.

In fact, slaves dominated plantation textile production in America during the eighteenth and early nineteenth centuries. Furthermore, while textile production was a male province in Africa, it became a female one in the new world, but one linked to the African heritage. This point is clearly stated by Maude Southwell Wahlman and Ellen King Torray in an article titled "Black American Folk Art: Quilts":

> The original link between African and Afro-American textile traditions was forged during the 300-year period in which Africans were brought to the United States as slaves.

15. A child's petticoat made in 1859 by a Negro seamstress. The skirt is gathered onto a plain bodice and features eyelet-embroidered circles centered with flowers, above which are rows of tucks. (Charleston Museum, Charleston, South Carolina)

14. A linen nightshirt that was made for Andrew Jackson by the slave, Gracey, c. 1830. (Courtesy The Ladies' Hermitage Association, Hermitage, Tennessee)

16. Two-piece jockey suit, handmade by plantation tailors in Waccamaw, South Carolina, in the early 1800s. Jacket of red and dark-green satin stripes with white buckskin trousers. (Charleston Museum, Charleston, South Carolina)

Although men had traditionally been the textile artists in Africa, American plantation owners adhered to the European system of labor division. Thus, Black women became the principal weavers, seamstresses, and quilters in Southern society. Quilts were produced by Black women for utilitarian and decorative purposes in both White and Black households. Quilts made for Whites are hardly distinguishable from traditional Anglo-American ones. However, those quilts made for the personal use of Blacks (very few examples survive) were designed and stitched in the African tradition. Black women preserved these African textile traditions and passed them on from generation to generation over several hundred years. Many contemporary Afro-American quilters are unaware of this sense of continuity, but the design similarities between their work and tradi-

tional African textiles are so close as to prompt some historical explanation.[2]

A similar point is made by James E. Newton in "Slave Artisans and Craftsmen: The Roots of Afro-American Art":

Black women on Southern Plantations made cloth from cotton and wool from which clothing was made. The women dominated the sewing and dressmaking arts and provided the plantation, especially the mistresses, with delicate needle and handiwork. One slave seamstress Elizabeth Keckly used her sewing ability to buy her freedom and later became a prominent dressmaker in Washington, D.C. where she eventually became dressmaker for Mrs. Abraham Lincoln. At formal functions the First Lady wore many garments donned by Mrs. Keckly, while at times Mr. Lincoln "sported" the William Fleurville, generally known as "Billy the Barber."[3]

17. Three-piece blue wool suit made by the slaves of Andrew Jackson Grayson of Bland County, Virginia. Grayson was a captain of F Company, 45th Regiment, Virginia Infantry. (The Museum of the Confederacy, Richmond, Virginia)

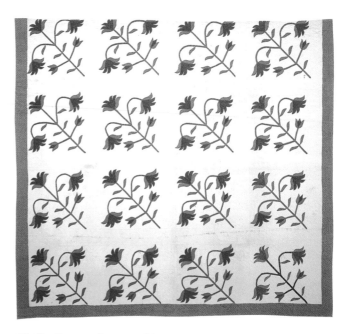

18, 19. Two quilts pieced by Mrs. Cynthia Evelyn Bush and quilted by her twin slave seamstresses, Frances and Ellen. Frances's husband, a barber, eventually purchased her freedom for $2,000. One of these quilts won First Prize at the first Noxubee County Fair. (Private collection; photograph courtesy Mississippi State Historical Museum, Jackson, Mississippi)

As Mary Todd Lincoln's seamstress, Mrs. Keckly stitched a quilt that still survives, presumably made from pieces of Mrs. Lincoln's dresses. In her 1868 autobiography *Behind the Scenes*, Mrs. Keckly explains how she was able to purchase her freedom and that of her son using money earned through her sewing skills.

A number of other slave women were able to purchase their freedom as a direct result of income earned from sewing skills. For example, Lucy A. Delaney, whose nineteenth-century autobiography *From the Darkness Cometh the Light* or *Struggles for Freedom* (privately printed in 1890 by the publishing house of J. T. Smith, St. Louis, Missouri), described the roles sewing skills played in enabling both her and her mother to purchase their freedom.

More opportunities to earn extra income were but one benefit that accrued to slave artisans, who held an important place in plantation hierarchy: they also were better fed, clothed, and housed, and had more freedom of movement.

The importance of becoming a plantation seamstress is reflected in the efforts of Nancy Dodson to become one:

> At 16 [Nancy Dodson] was sent to Mrs. Jones' home to learn to be a tailoress. Nancy remained for a year or two but instead of being taught her trade she was made to do general housework and mind the child.

Sometimes she seamed a seam but she was bright enough to see that this would not make a "seamster" of her and she began to yearn for her home.

One day the overseer sent some cloth for Nancy to cut a coat—he wanted to see how much she had learned—Mrs. Jones say nothing to Nancy, but took the cloth, cut the coat and partly made it—basted the other seams and gave them to Nancy to sew while she went out to pass the evening with the neighbor—no sooner had she gone than Nancy rolled up the coat and ran away home with it. As soon as the overseer saw her he asked her if she could undertake to cut out some cloth for the hands—Nancy replied "I have a pattern and I can make them by it." She sat up that night and ripped the coat all apart, cut an exact pattern and then put it together again. She did the same with pants and vests and then she undertook her *trade*. From this time she made and superintended the making *of all the clothing*—pants, coats, vests, shirts, etc. for all the men and boys on two large farms.[4]

20. This silver cup was awarded to the First Prize quilt at the first Noxubee County Fair. See figures 18, 19. (Private collection; photograph courtesy Mississippi State Historical Museum, Jackson, Mississippi)

On many plantations full-time seamstresses made garments for male and female slaves (including children). As one ex-slave described these artisans, "Regular women done our quiltings and made our dresses. She made our dresses plain waist, full gathered skirt and buttons down the backs of our waist."[5] In this instance, "regular" meant that these women were assigned to work as seamstresses. In addition to dresses, the seamstresses also made jackets, men's trousers (pantaloons), quilts, coverlets, and table linens. Quilting was not confined to bed covers. Slave seamstresses also quilted petticoats, outer skirts, and pants.

Historical records indicate that slave women operated on a task system, as the following 1849 diary entry suggests:

> Sarah has made this year in May 3 pairs of mens pantaloons in a day—and made well also 3 dresses for women
>
> Her task is 2½ pairs of pants or 2½ chemises or 2½ dresses for women per day
>
> Jenny Young makes 2 pr pants and shirts or makes 2 chemises or 2 dresses for women[6]

The amount of work required of the slave seamstresses depended on the plantation clothes allowance. According to Ulrich Bonnell Phillips in *American Negro Slavery*, slaves received specific allotments:

> Hammond's clothing allowance was for each man in the fall two cotton shirts, a pair of woolen pants and a woolen jacket, and in the spring two cotton shirts and two pairs of cotton pants, with privilege of substitution when desired; for each woman six yards of woolen cloth and six yards of cotton in the fall, six yards of light and six of heavy cotton cloth in the spring, with needles, thread and buttons on each occasion. Each worker was to have a pair of stout shoes in the fall, and a heavy blanket every third year. Children's cloth allowances were proportionate and their mothers were required to dress them in clean clothes twice a week.[7]

The scheduling of sewing duties for the plantation seamstresses depended, for the most part, on the size of the plantation. On large plantations cutting and sewing continued year round. On smaller plantations, this activity was confined to the slow season. Margaret Thompson Ordonez observed:

> Construction of garments could have been either a slack period or a year-round activity. On the Edward Bradford plantation, Eppes recalled that eight seamstresses were given pieces of fabrics to sew into garments in the slave quarters. The cutting of the garment pieces had been supervised closely by the owner's wife, probably to insure accuracy and the best utilization of the fabric. This was repeated week after week, year in and year out....
>
> On the Chemonie plantation in 1841, "making Negro Clothing" was a task assigned to 1 or 2 persons from April intermittently through June and again in December.[8]

In some instances plantation owners adhered to a rigid scheduling:

> Twice a year each slave had two new suits of clothes. In the spring the men obtained two

pairs of pants, two shirts, and a straw hat; in the fall, two more pairs of pants and shirts, a coat, and a woolen hat. Semiannually the women donned new dresses and "linins." According to the Tait records, this did not mean that on two days of each year every slave issued from his cabin resplendent from crown to toe in new garments. In the spring of 1861, nearly a month (April 6 to May 3) elapsed between the time the first men and the last received pantaloons. Issuing the shirts required an even longer time, May 13 to June 19. The fall interval was prolonged even longer, the first coat being issued on September 12 and the last one on November 19. Much time was required for the several seamstresses to make four to five garments apiece for more than sixty slaves.[9]

21, 22, 23, 24, 25, 26. These six quilts are said to have been made by "sewing women"—slaves that were specially trained to do quilting. (Collection of Mary Alden Carrison, Rembert, South Carolina)

22

23

24

The correlation between sewing skills and quilting was understood, with slave seamstresses making many of the plantation quilts. An Arkansas ex-slave reported: "I lived near Coffeyville in Upshaw County. That's whar my husband found me. I was living with my aunt and uncle. They said the reason I had such a good gift makin' quilts was cause my mother was a seamstress."[10]

Further evidence is offered by another slave who stated:

> Lucy was a pretty mulatto girl about twenty years old. She sewed for the Cheatham family and was allowed to visit her mother every evening at the slave quarters. Father went down to her mother's cabin. A candle was burning on the table inside and he could see the old woman and Lucy at work on a patchwork quilt.[11]

Slave seamstresses who became passionate quilters considered the craft an "ongoing one." Every spare moment was devoted to the craft. "Miss, I weren't born to be lazy, I weren't raised dat wey, and I sho ain't skeered to die."[12] An Arkansas slave remembered: "I used to quilt until my fingers got too stiff."[13]

A former Georgia slave describes another slave's pride in her quilt-making skills.

> Nancy was proud of her quilt-making ability. "Git 'um, Vanna, let de ladies see 'um," she said; and when Vanna brought the gay pieces made up in a "double-burst" (sunburst) pattern, Nancy fingered the squares with loving fingers. "Hit's poetry, ain't it?" she asked wistfully, "I made one for a white lady two years ago, but dey hurst my fingers now—makes 'em stiff."[14]

An Arkansas slave observed, "They made awful close stitches and backstitched every now and then to make it hold. They would wax the thread to keep it from rolling up and tangling."[15]

A similar point was made by the granddaughter of Helen Mary Kirkpatrick Tinnin (an early nineteenth-century Texas pioneer) concerning slave stitches:

> Still in the possession of her granddaughter and namesake, Miss Helen Tinnin, are two of the fine linen sheets made by the slaves.
>
> The flax for these sheets was planted at Helen Mary's direction in the low-lying areas along the river. The sheets were woven on the plantation itself. How well she instructed her slaves is shown by the tiny hems and stitches so beautifully done.[16]

25

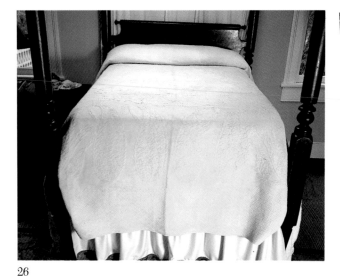

26

27. A nineteenth-century slave-made quilt from Monroeville, Alabama. (Cincinnati Art Museum, Cincinnati, Ohio; Gift of Mr. and Mrs. Cletus T. Palmer)

Sewing skills were among the trades taught to slaves, depending on several factors: the size of the plantation, the degree to which the plantation wished to be self-sufficient, the craft of their masters.

> The trades which were taught the slaves depended no little on the necessities of the plantation or the crafts of their most intelligent slave youths to train as artisans that they might supply the needs of the self-sufficient plantations. Accordingly, on every large plantation could be found the Negro carpenter, blacksmith, and stone mason, weaver, seamstress, cabinet maker, cooper, sawyer, shoemaker, etc.[17]

28. A Broderie Perse quilt that is elaborately appliquéd with chintz cutouts, c. 1810. The quilting covers the entire surface and in most places it is no more than an eighth of an inch apart. This beautiful piece was made by Kadella, who had been purchased by Colonel John Carson at the slave market in Charleston, South Carolina. Alleged to have been his

mistress, Kadella lived in a special house that Carson built across a creek from the other slave quarters. Kadella was said to have been a princess from Barbados, and she spent all her time sewing and quilting. According to tradition, she was so loved and respected by the other slaves that they transported her in a rickshaw. (Carson House, Old Fort, North Carolina)

28a. Detail of the Broderie Perse quilt made by Kadella. (Carson House, Old Fort, North Carolina)

29. Detail of a Star quilt made c. 1850 by Kadella's daughter, Sara, who was a plantation seamstress at Carson House. Later, Sara moved to Charlotte, North Carolina, to live with Colonel Carson's daughter, and in 1890 she died and is buried in Charlotte. (Carson House, Old Fort, North Carolina)

30. The Carson House in Old Fort, North Carolina. Begun as a two-story log house in 1793, two more rooms and a dog trot were added later, and a third story followed. The front and back porches, which run the length of the house, were the last additions.

But the demand for skilled seamstresses was so great that nineteenth-century Southern newspapers regularly advertised for skilled female slaves, primarily seamstresses. These ads requested either a "plain" or a "complete" seamstress, which suggested an artisan who was proficient not only in cutting and sewing but also in embroidery and other similar skills.

> The term "complete" workman was applied to many Negroes, including a woman considered to be a "complete Seamstress and House Servant" and a man referred to as a "complete House Painter and Glazier." A female slave was praised as being "fit for country or city Business," since she could cord, spin and knit rather well....Placed on a par with any worker, regardless of color, was a girl of "very superior qualifications." As described by her master in the slave's advertisement, "I venture to say that there is not a better seamstress, cutter and fitter of ladies' and children's dresses..., or a more fanciful netter of beadbags, money purses, etc."[18]

31. Detail of a Crazy quilt. In 1842, John Logan put Hannah, a twelve-year-old slave girl, behind his daughter on her wedding day, and then put Pharoh, a twelve-year-old slave boy, behind his new son-in-law. Then John Logan said, "These are your wedding gifts." Hannah became a house servant and Pharoh became a blacksmith. They later married and had a daughter, Emma. Hannah made quilts, and she worked on this Crazy quilt before the Civil War. She died before completing it. The quilt was finished by Emma in 1895, and one corner of the quilt is inscribed, "Finished by M." (Carson House, Old Fort, North Carolina)

32. Grove Hill, also known as the Bradsher house or the T. Y. Greenlee house, after Thomas Young Greenlee. This log house was built in 1843 in Old Fort, North Carolina. It was here that Hannah, who began the Crazy quilt illustrated in figure 31, worked as a house servant.

33. Broderie Perse quilt made by Johanna Davis, who was at least thirteen years old when she made it, probably between 1845 and 1853, when her first child, Susan A. Davis, was born. Johanna Davis, who was a skilled mantua maker and dressmaker, may have been a free black artisan rather than a slave. (Avery Institute, College of Charleston, South Carolina)

More often, however, an advertisement had to be inserted in the newspapers. These notices were very similar to sales listings in their description of the slave's talents.

"To be hired immediately," a typical advertisement stated, "A very complete Seamstress; a complete worker of muslin, sober, and no runaway; she is a young colored Woman in her eighteenth year; she is very fond of children, can make their clothes [sic] and dress them with taste." Another master, apparently anxious to make a profit as soon as possible, offered an eight-year-old girl who was "very smart at her needle" and could do all forms of housework.[19]

Slave girls as young as eight and up were the subject of these pre–Civil War ads: "a twelve-year-old girl who was handy with a needle and had been trained as a mantua [loose gown] maker."[20]

An analysis of probate wills reveals that some plantation owners were concerned about the future of their slaves, and in some cases stipulated training in sewing as a means by which these slaves could become independent. The will of David Brown of Somerset County, Maryland, dated July 19, 1697, is an example:

...its my Will that Black Beetee be larned to read the bible and to Sowe with Needle well to have good Cloaths and two Cowes and Calves When set free Which I desire to be at the twenty Second yeare of her Age She being Eight yeares of age Last Apprill and I Desire that her Mother black Pegg Shall Serve twelve yeares after my Decease And then to be Sett free.[21]

The will of Thomas Fluornoy also demonstrates this concern for the future of his slaves:

The will of Thomas Fluornoy, of Powhatan county, probated in 1795, emancipated all of his slaves and directed that his executors should secure certificates of emancipation from the court. The males under twenty-one years of age were to be bound to some industrious mechanic to learn a trade and to remain so bound until they reached the age of twenty-one; and the females under eighteen years of age to some industrious person to learn to sew, spin and weave, until they became eighteen years of age.[22]

Additionally, household inventories of the nineteenth century contain information regarding African-American seamstresses, including former slaves who had earned their freedom. A case in point is Amanda Cousins of Richmond, Virginia:

The will and household inventory of Amanda Cousins, a free black seamstress in Richmond, indicated a modest level of prosperity which she shared by raising the children of a deceased cousin. The inventory also reveals that she lent money to neighbors and held their promissory notes. Of the approximately 600 adult free black women in Richmond in 1852, the city directory lists ten cooks, 65 seamstresses, and 132 laundresses.[23]

A careful analysis of Miss Cousins's household inventory reveals that she had amassed considerable material goods. Interestingly enough, two quilts listed

35. Silk quilt made 1837-1850 in the Touching Stars pattern by Aunt Ellen and Aunt Margaret, who were slaves of the Marmaduke Beckwith Morton family at The Knob, near Russellville, Logan County, Kentucky. The quilt is a masterpiece of fine piecing, quilting, and stuffed work featuring a variety of plants. Aunt Ellen and Aunt Margaret remained with the Morton family after Emancipation and died at The Knob. (The Metropolitan Museum of Art, New York; Gift of Roger Morton and Dr. Paul C. Morton, 1962)

City of Richmond, to wit

We the undersigned agreably to the annexed order of Court, having been first duly sworn, according to law for that purpose, do hereby certify that we have to the best of our judgements appraised the personal estate of Amanda Cousins, late of this City, deceased, and have fixed the value to the same, and herewith return the said appraisement under our hands to the Court in order that the same may be recorded, Given under our hands, this 26th day of September 1860, as follows, to wit

		$	¢
	1 Watch	10	"
	1 Gold Chain	12	"
	1 Silver Cup & Sugar Tongs & Spoon	2	"
	1 Cameo Breastpin	1	"
	1 Pair Ear rings & thimble	"	50
	Lot of Studs, Rings &c	2	"
Room No 1	1 Bedstead & 2 Mattresses	15	"
	1 Marble Top Table	5	"
	Pitchers, Basins &c	1	"
	1 Bureau, Marble top	10	"
	1 Hair Sofa	10	"
	1 Lounge	3	"
	1 Small Table	2	"
	3 Window Shades	1	50
	2 Lamps	"	75
	Fire Screen	"	25
	1 Oil Can	"	20
" No 2	1 Wardrobe	35	"
	1 Cabinet	20	"
	Carried forward	131	20

36. Partial inventory, dated July 1, 1860, of the estate of Amanda Cousins, a free black seamstress. Such inventories provide valuable historical evidence in researching nineteenth-century women. (Will Book, Richmond Circuit Court, Virginia)

in the sale of her general estate were not included in her inventory.

Some cities, such as Charleston, South Carolina, and Baltimore, Maryland, opened special schools to teach young African-American girls to sew and to learn decorative crafts like embroidery. The *City Gazette and Daily Advertiser* of Charleston, South Carolina, ran an advertisement for such a school on February 2, 1801:

Madam Marineau, widow of the late Mr. Marineau, who lately kept school in this city, has the honor to inform the Public, that on the 4th day of this instant, February, she proposes to open a School, for the education of Young Girls of Colour, she will learn them to Read, Write, Sew and Embroider. She hopes to merit the esteem and the confidence of the parents, by the care she will take that the children may profit by their lessons.

She resides at Mr. La de Vezis's, Merchant King Street, No. 85.[24]

There is sufficient historical evidence to support the supervisory role of the plantation mistress, and to a lesser extent, the wife of the overseer, in the production of plantation textiles. Additional evidence supports the view that Old Miss performed some of the labor required to produce garments for the big house and slave quarters, as well as bed coverings. But it should be noted that the bulk of textile production in the antebellum South was accomplished by the labor of slave men and women.

Plantation mistresses often supervised the production of clothing and some worked hard themselves in the actual production. On some of the large plantations a few slave women specialized in making clothes for all. But with or without the direction and assistance of the mistress and the slave seamstresses, the field women had to do extra work to provide some of their family's clothing, as well as to wash it and keep it in good repair.[25]

Still, the mistress performed a variety of tasks, especially on farms and smaller plantations. In some cases, she sewed the garments that were cut out by slave seamstresses.

38. Appliqué quilt made around 1840 by a sixteen-year-old slave on the plantation of Captain and Mrs. William Womack, Pittsylvania County, Virginia. (Smithsonian Institution, Washington, D.C.)

37. Slave-made appliqué quilt from the Cogburn Plantation near Montgomery, Alabama, 1830–1850. (Mississippi State Historical Museum, Jackson, Mississippi)

39. Slave-made appliqué quilt, Princess Feather pattern, c. 1820. Brought to Hinds County, Mississippi, around 1820 by the Lewis family of North Carolina. (Mississippi State Historical Museum, Jackson, Mississippi)

41. Pieced quilt, Rose pattern, possibly produced by slaves under the direction of Mrs. David Batey, Murfreesboro, Tennessee, 1862–1870. (Tennessee State Museum, Nashville, Tennessee)

40. "Jackson Hill" quilt, made by slaves for Mrs. Green Hill Jordan at Jackson Hill near Milledgeville, Georgia, 1820–1830. (The Atlanta Historical Society, Atlanta, Georgia)

42. Detail of a pieced Star quilt made by a slave near Macon, Georgia. (Old Slave Mart, Charleston, South Carolina)

43. Slave-made whole-cloth quilt, c. 1850. (The Atlanta Historical Society, Atlanta, Georgia)

44. This handsewn, white, plain-woven cotton homespun wedding dress was made for slave Sarah Tate around 1845 by her young mistress. It is touching evidence of the rapport that existed between some mistresses and their slaves. Sarah treasured the dress until the day she died at nearly one hundred years of age. Sarah had been brought to Texas with her daughter by the Edgar family of Concrete, DeWitt County. (San Antonio Museum Association, San Antonio, Texas)

Evidence indicates that women slaves handled most of the work done on clothing construction. When the time came for actual sewing, however, white mistresses or overseers' wives often assumed the position of head seamstress. In a letter dated November 13, 1831, Rachel O'Connor of Francisville wrote her sister, Mrs. Mary Weeks of New Iberia, Louisiana, that "Clarisse's illness prevented me from getting the Negro clothing fixed as early in the year, as I commonly do, for them. However am pretty well through with it at last." A later letter dated May 23, 1842, from Rachel tells Mrs. Mary C. Moore that "I should like to have the cloth sent before the weather gets very cold so that I may get my part of the work done when I am able to work."[26]

And occasionally the mistress both cut and sewed slave garments:

—went to see about the carpenters working at the negro houses, where there are men mending chimneys, white washing, & these carpenters Grimball told me he wished me to see about every day, & now I have to cut out flannel jackets, and alter some work.[27]

Though much sewing was still done by hand, the advent of the sewing machine lightened the load for both mistress and slave seamstresses alike:

The first sewing machine that was ever bought in Travis County was purchased by the Tinnins. Helen Mary undertook to teach one of the house servants, Old Aunt Rose, how to use it. The old Negro woman then taught other women slaves. All of the clothes worn by the slaves on the plantations were made by the slave women on Helen Mary's "first" machine. Helen Mary also taught the women how to sew by hand.[28]

Some advertisers in nineteenth-century newspapers boasted about the aptitude of their slaves on the sewing machine and offered testimonials:

The invention of the sewing machine speeded up production of garments on plantations, and slaves sometimes operated the machines. Several sewing machine advertisements in the Tallahassee newspaper promoted the use of the machines for slave clothes. A testimonial from Dr. R. W. Fisher stated: "Most of my sewing on my plantation is done by a *negro girl* not *fourteen* years old...."[29]

But of special interest to us in this book is the role of the plantation mistress with regard to slave quilting. By some accounts, she cut out quilt patterns, then turned the piecing and actual quilting over to slave labor. This view is supported by the following comment from an ex-slave: "Miss Cornelia cut me some quilt pieces. She say 'Betty that's her talent' bout me. Miss Betty say, 'If she goin' to be mine I want her to be smart.'"[30] Other accounts suggest that the mistress allowed the slaves to do the piecing, but preferred to do the stitching herself.

Undervalued is the mutuality and sharing of the sewing skills, design concepts, and sense of color in textile production. Old Miss and slave learned from each other, alternating the roles of teacher and student. A WPA interviewer described a slave who had learned sewing skills from the mistress: "Harriett Greeham...sits on the porch of her shabby cottage and sews the stitches that were taught her by her mistress...."[31]

Sometimes, the mistress made an entire quilt for slave use. As one ex-slave recalled, "I had just a little straw tick and a cot that de massa made himself and I had a common quilt dat de missus made to cover me."[32]

45. This quilt top is from Darsyton Hall Plantation in South Carolina. A note with the quilt top states that it was made by a Negro seamstress in 1780, but the fabrics used suggest that it was actually made in the early 1800s. (The American Museum in Britain, Bath, England)

46. Jane Arthur Bond (Courtesy the Pennington Family)

The abundance of historical documentation—written records, family papers, family recollections and reminiscences, artifacts, and photographs—concerning the life of Jane Arthur Bond is staggering when compared to the dearth of these sources for the majority of slave quilters.

Jane Bond was born into slavery in Knox County (now Bell County), Kentucky, in 1828. Originally the property of Edward Fletcher Arthur, Jane was given as a wedding present to his daughter, Belinda, when she married a Methodist minister, Preston Bond, in 1848. However, tensions developed early between the two women and were exacerbated by the birth of Jane's two sons fathered by Preston Bond.

As a means of easing the situation, Jane was given a second time as a wedding present to Preston Bond's sister, Rebecca, in celebration of her marriage to Peter Routt, a local Kentucky farmer. Happily, Rebecca and Jane formed a close friendship and shared many experiences, including quilting. The three quilts illustrated here were made by these two women.

After the Civil War, Jane and her two sons returned to her original owner, Edward Fletcher Arthur, and his wife Susan Emma Routt Arthur. Jane and Susan quilted together in this postwar period. According to family history, it was Jane who taught Susan how to quilt, and approximately twenty of their quilts have survived.

Julian Bond is a present-day descendant of this family. For additional information see *The Bonds: An American Family*, by Roger M. Williams.

48. Quilt made by Jane Arthur Bond and Rebecca Bond Routt.

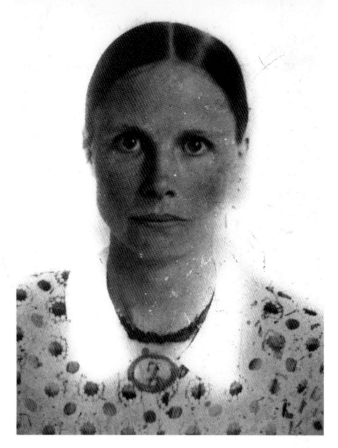

47. Rebecca Bond Routt (Courtesy the Pennington Family)

49. Quilt made by Jane Arthur Bond and Rebecca Bond Routt.

50. Quilt made by Jane Arthur Bond and Rebecca Bond Routt.

There can be no apology for the harshness and brutality of slavery. But occasionally, both slave women and plantation mistresses managed to transcend their circumstances and develop a very special relationship. Sewing was often the catalyst that brought them together.

> My mistress was so kind to me that I was always glad to do her bidding and proud to labor for her as much as my young years would permit....Would sit by her side for hours sewing diligently, with a heart as free from care as that of any freeborn white child. When she thought I was tired, she would send me out to run and jump, and away I bounded to gather berries or flowers to decorate her room. Those were happy days—too happy to last.[33]

The mistress could be a powerful friend. Her encouragement and support could mean privileged status for a few skilled slaves. The life of Ellen Craft is an example.

Her mistress did, however, encourage one of Ellen's talents—sewing. Ready-made clothing and sewing machines were still in the future, so that Ellen's skill with a needle was an important asset, particularly after the Collinses' first baby was born. By the 1840s Ellen was spending most of her time as a seamstress. She was permitted to move to a one-room cabin of her own, in the woods behind the big house, where she could keep bolts of cloth and sewing implements. There she had some measure of privacy.[34]

The mistress could also be a powerful enemy. Many slaves, including skilled needle workers, were sold because of the perception of rebelliousness. In the following example, even the embroidery skills of this slave failed to save her from the wrath of her mistress:

> A girl that had been brought up in all respects "like a lady," she could embroider and play on the piano, and dress like a lady, and read, and write, and dance, and all this she had learned in the family which had brought them up, and who had treated her in her childhood as if she had been their own. But, however, her mind had grown too high for her; she had become proud, and now to humble her, they had brought her here to be sold.[35]

Some mistresses were generally dissatisfied with all of their slave house servants. This dissatisfaction extended even to accusations of theft of cloth:

> Mrs. Medlock complains bitterly of our servants, with what justice I do not pretend to enquire, as I requested her, at the first, to force them to do right, while they were in the back yard. She say Hetty makes great threats in the kitchen, and that Mary Ann is the most impudent creature she ever saw. She specified several sorts of misconduct. She was charged by Anna too, while we were there, with stealing 12 or 14 yards of domestic, tho' I feel no uneasiness about that, disbelieving it, entirely, for many reasons. Anna's proof was only in her negro woman, who is utterly unprincipled, as we all know, always. Be it as it may, my comfort is disturbed by such things, and I am sorry to hear them.[36]

Larger plantations in the antebellum South had specially equipped dependency buildings known as "sewing houses" or "loom rooms," in which all the sewing, quilting, and weaving took place. The design of these buildings and the materials used to make them

51. A loom house used by slaves at Prestwould Plantation, Macklenburg County, Virginia. (Photograph by Willie Graham, The Colonial Williamsburg Foundation, Williamsburg, Virginia)

52. Loom house used by slaves in Isle of Wight County, Virginia.

were regionally determined. Three distinct areas can be identified: tidewater, low country, and deep South.

Multi-use separate kitchens and storage buildings were used for sewing and related activities when no special facility was provided. In the deep South, primarily Louisiana, porches (known locally as galleries) that extended the length of the house, front and back, were also used for textile production.

QUILTING IN THE QUARTERS

Mr. House did not give blankets, the slaves were required to make the necessary cover by piecing together left over goods. After this process was completed, it was padded with cotton and then dyed in much the same way as homespun. After the dyeing was completed the slave was the owner of a new quilt.[1]

It has been commonly thought that slaves in the general plantation population didn't quilt. After all, working in the fields all day would have left them too little time or too little energy at night for such activity. Besides, where would they get fabric with which to quilt?

Such a view is reflected by Abigail Curlee in her dissertation, *A Study of Texas Slave Plantations, 1822-1865:* "The Negroes used blankets for bed-cover, but records are meager. Some quilts may have been made and used." Given the general historical silence on this subject, such a view is, at least, charitable.

53. Pieced quilt of the late 1700s, which makes it the oldest quilt in this book. The fabrics used in the quilt might well have been woven on a plantation. (The Valentine Museum, Richmond, Virginia)

54. Appliqué crib quilt created with textiles that slaves made for their own use, c. 1850. The appliqué top is not made from fine cotton, the backing is homespun, and seeds remain in the cotton batting. (Collection of Eleanor Lee, Woodstock, New York)

55. Appliqué quilt by Jane Batson, a Virginia-born slave, c. 1850, depicting elaborately costumed men and women. One of the most interesting aspects of this quilt is the use of pink fabric rather than black for the faces of the figures. Black images are known to have been used on nineteenth-century quilts, but the practice appears to have been more common among white quilters. Of course, it is possible that the quilt had been originally intended for a white person, but for some reason it remained in the Batson family, for it was worked on at a later date by Jane Batson's niece. (Courtesy Marcia Spark, Tucson, Arizona)

Subsequent research has shown that slaves made two types of quilts: those for their personal use, made on their own time; and quilts for the big house, stitched under the supervision of the mistress.

The number of surviving quilts made by slaves for their own use on their own time is astonishingly small. Many factors contributed to their destruction, beginning with the increased mobility brought about by the emancipation of slaves. With each move, the possibility of losing personal possessions, such as quilts, increased. Personal possessions often got left behind when slaves moved:

> When we started from Mississippi, dey tol' us de Yankees 'ud kill us iffen dey foun' us and dey say, "You ain't got no time to take nothin' to wher you goin." Take your little bundle and lev all you has in your house. So when we got to Texas I jus' one dress, what I had en. Dat's de way all de cullud people was fer freedom, never had nothin' but what had on de back. Some of dem had right smart in dere cabins, but they was skeered and day lef' everything. Bed clothes and all you had was lef'. We didn' know any better den.[2]

Fire, theft, and sale for extra income also contributed to the disappearance of these quilts, but frequent use was perhaps the most important factor. Few options are available to people of reduced means: a bed cover, no matter how special, had to be used.

The loss due to fire was best summed up in the following testimony: "I had thirty-five quilts to get burnt up and eleven woolen blankets and my burial clothes all got burnt up too."[3]

Theft of Southern household goods by Northern

56, 57, 58, 58a. These three quilts made by slave Nancy Vaughn Ford are important, for they are good examples of the utilitarian quilts made by slaves for their own use in their free time. In the detail illustration (58a) of figure 58 it is possible to see the blue knitted section that has been incorporated in the quilt. Although slaves knitted continuously, little of this kind of work survives. (Courtesy the McIntosh family)

soldiers was rampant. "They [Yankees] took everything. They took all Miss Betty's nice silverware. They took fine quilts and feather beds. Dey searched de houses an' took de things."[4]

Other ex-slaves recalled:

> When dem Yankees cum up ter de house I wus mi'ty skeered. I got b'hind old granny's skirt an' niver let dem see me. Dey wint in de big house an' took de new quilts and counterpins an' put dem under deir saddles; dey burnt de gin an' all de cotton on de place, an' scattered all do corn out uf de crib, an' I had ter he'p pick up hut dey left.[5]

Still another account noted:

> I never will forgit how bad dem yankees treated Old Miss. Dey stole all her good hosses, and her chickens and dey broke in de smokehouse end tuk her meat. Dey went in de big house and tuk her nice quilts and blankets. She stood all of dat wid a straightface but when dey foun' her gold, she just broke down and cried and cried. I stayed on and was Miss Annie's houseboy long as she lasted. I was twenty-one when she died.[6]

57

58

58a

Further destruction of textiles was indicated by the comment: "My pappy helped at de hospital after dat battle, and dey has it in a hotel and makes bandages out of sheets and pillow cases and underwear, and uses de rugs and carpets for quilts."[7]

But day-in, day-out use wore out most of the quilts. Just keeping them clean was a major element in their destruction. Saturday was the official wash day on most plantations when slaves were required to wash their clothes and bed linens. The process was time consuming, tedious, and extremely hard on textiles.

First, all soiled clothes were placed outdoors in an iron pot. Where no pots were available, other types of vessels were used:

> We had no tubs either, so father took a hollow log and split it open and put partitions in it. He bored a hole in each section and drove a peg in it. He next cut two forked poles and drove 'em in de ground and rested de ends of de hollow

log in dese forks. We'd fill de log trough wid water and rinse our clothes. We could pull out de pegs and let de water out. We had no brooms either, so we made brush brooms to sweep our floors.[8]

A fire was lit under the pit and the clothes were boiled with homemade lye soap:

> The usual laundry and toilet soap was a homemade lye product, some of it a soft-solid, and some as liquid as water. The latter was stored in jugs and demijohns. Either would "fetch the dirt, or take the hide off"; in short, when applied "with rag and water, something had to come."[9]

The wash was then beaten (to loosen dirt) with a special board or "battlin stick," or simply "tromped by children in their bare feet."

> Wen we uster wash quilts we uster cut a stick and after dat made de tub, den my Mammy would put water in dese tubs den soft soap de quilts den us chilluns would git in de tubs in our bare foots en tromp de dirt out.[10]

Very few quilts could survive this trauma, and few did!

The quilts they made were central to the lives of many slaves, and they were used in a variety of ways. Their most important function was as bed covers.

Slaves described two types of beds: ones with wooden frames on which slates were nailed to beds, and beds attached to the wall. An ex-slave from Georgia described the latter:

> The beds used by most of the slaves in that day and time were called "Georgia beds," and these were made by boring two holes in the cabin wall, and two in the floor, and side pieces were run from the holes in the wall to the posts and fastened; then planks were nailed around the sides and foot, box-fashion, to hold in the straw that we used for mattresses; over this pretty white sheets and plenty of quilts was spreaded. Yes, maam, there was always plenty of good warm cover in those days. Of course, it was home-made, all of it.[11]

Another version of an attached bed was described in the following manner:

> De bed was one-legged and hit was made in de corner of de room, wid de leg settin' out in de middle of de flo'. A plank was runned

'twix' de logs of de cabin an' nailed to de post on de front of de bed. Across de foot an' udder plank was runned into de logs an' nail' to de legs. Den some straw or cornshucks was piled on for a mattress. Us used anythang what we could git for kivver.[12]

Although children usually slept on the floor, underneath the larger beds were sometimes trundle beds for children.

Made by the plantation carpenter and blacksmith, wooden beds were held together by cords rather than bedsprings. One ex-slave commented, "You had to be mighty careful tightenin' dem cords or de beds was liable to fall down."[13]

Cowhide covered the bed cording, and on top of it was placed a mattress made out of "wheat straw," which the slaves referred to as "Georgy feathers." The straw was changed yearly: "When they threshed every year, they throwed that old straw out and put new in."[14]

Less frequently used were mattresses filled with cornshucks. In some instances, a separate "feather mattress" was placed on top of the straw. Other slaves survived on mattresses made out of gunny sacks filled with leaves.

White or striped coarse homespun covered the mattresses. Sheets were made from unbleached homespun: "Dem sheets wuz biled wi'd hand-made soap whit kept 'em white lak dat."[15]

Quilts, counterpanes, or coverlets served as bed coverings, though some slaves had a different experience: "I can remember when we thought a newspaper opened out was a bed cover."[16]

Slaves also used quilts as makeshift beds or pallets. Adult slaves defined pallets as a "quilt or tow [torn] carpet spread in de floor" and used them in their cabins when no other beds were available. And pallets were used by slaves when they were required to spend the night in the plantation house. One ex-slave explained: "I always stayed in the 'big house,' slept on the floor, right near the fireplace, with one quilt for my bed and one quilt to cover me."[17]

Another one said: "I slept on de floor up at de 'big house' in de white woman's room on a quilt. I'd git up in de mornings, make fires, put on de coffee, and tend to my little brother. Jest do little odd jobs sech as that."[18]

Children almost always slept on pallets. One ex-slave explained: "They put a old quilt down on the floor for the li'l folks."[19] Another commented: "De sleepin' places wus bunks fer de grown niggers an de chillun slept on de floor on pallets."[20]

Nursing babies were carried by their mothers to the field. Between feedings, they were placed on pallets.

One ex-slave described this practice: "When de wimen who had babies wint to de fiel' dey took dem babies wid 'em, an' made a pallet out uf a old quilt in de fence corner, an' put dem babies dar while dey hoed and plowed."[21]

And: "Mammy Lit wud spread a quilt on de gallery [porch] an' put de babies on de floor an' we had to keep de chaps frum gittin' off de pallet an' rollin' off de gallery."[22]

In addition, quilts had a religious function. Nineteenth-century sources mention their use in baptismal ceremonies. Quilts frequently decorated grave sites in accordance with the African tradition that the last articles used by the deceased were placed on the grave.

Quilts also functioned in a variety of other ways—as substitutes for ironing boards, as cushions in the bottom of wagons or on wagon seats, as a carrying device for children, and as a means for hiding out.

Referring to the quilt as a hiding place, one ex-slave stated: "One day mammy come afte' me an I run an' hid under a pile of quilts an' laked to smothered to death wittin' for her to go on off."[23]

At the end of the Civil War, another ex-slave managed to escape on a train with three small children hidden in a quilt:

> But my sister stole us away. A white woman in another county hired my sister and gave her railroad fare to come to her place. My sister rolled up three of our baby sisters like a handle bundle in a quilt and told 'em don't move or cry and as soon as she could unroll 'em and let 'em have some air she would. So she got on de train with them three little niggers in a bundle and toted 'em up under her arms like dey was her clothes and belongings, and put 'em under her seat on de train. De bundle was so big every time de conductor passed it was in de way and he would kick it out of his way. Sister protected dem de best she could. Soon as he pass, she opened it and let 'em have some air. When she see him coming back, she wrap 'em up again. Dey was all sure glad to git off dat train.[24]

One ex-slave remembered with horror when her grandmother's baby (the ex-slave's father) fell out of a quilt:

> Grandma was walking long wid the hack and somewhere she cut through and climbed over a railin' fence. She lost her baby outer her quilts and went on a mile fore she knowed bout it. She say, "Lawd, Master Daniel, if I

ain't lost my baby." They stopped the hack and she went back to see where her baby could be. She knowed where she got out the hack and she knowed she had the baby then. Fore she got to the fence she clum over, she seed her baby on the snow. She said the sun was warm and he was well wrop up. That all what saved em. She shuck him round till she woke him up. She was so scared he be frozen. When he let out cryin' she knowed he be all right. She put in the foot of the hack among jugs of hot water what they had to keep em warm.[25]

Quilts are constructed for hard use. By definition, they have three layers: the top portion, which can be plain, pieced, or appliquéd; the middle layer (or filling); and the lining. Quilt stitches, or "tacking," bond these three layers together.

For the top portion, slaves used material left over from their plantation clothing allowance and old cast-off clothing, cut up and reused for quilt squares. Eighteenth- and nineteenth-century sources referred to homespun, linsey or linsey-woolsey, jean, ticking, osnaburg, and kersey, among other fabrics. Slaves also found a way to use gunny, feed, flour, tobacco, and sugar sacks. Additionally, slaves purchased new cloth, such as calico, flannel, broadcloth, and gingham from extra income.

The ingenuity with which slaves used "throw away" or discarded goods is astonishing. For example, a Georgia slave said: "Grandma brought her feather bed wid her from Virginny, and she used to piece up a heap of quilts outen our ole clo'es and any kind of scraps she could get a holt of."[26] Louise J. Evans, an ex-slave from South Carolina, remembers using another type of discarded goods: "I used to wait on the girl who did the weavin'. When she took the cloth off the loom she done give me the 'thrums [ends of thread left on the loom]."[27]

For the middle layer, or filling, slaves used clothes that could no longer be mended, leftover threads from the loom, pieces of raw cotton, and bits and pieces of wool. An Arkansas ex-slave described the latter use: "They carded and washed the sheep's wool and put it in their quilts."[28] This practice was also described by another ex-slave:

> While dey is haulin', de women make quilts and dey is wool quilts. Course, dey ain't made out of shearin' wool, but jes' as good. Marse John have lots of sheep and when dey go through de briar patch de wool cotch on dem briars and in de fall de women folks goes out and picks de wool off de briars jes' like you

59. This crib quilt, made in an original pattern showing strong African influence, was made in the period 1840–1860. According to Dr. Robert Farris Thompson of Yale University, the three motifs on the quilt—coffins, crosses, and suns—suggest that the quilt was made as a memorial for a dead child or as an amulet to ensure renewed health for a sick child. Red and white are also the colors of Shango, a religious cult that originated in Nigeria and spread to the New World. The crosses and suns on this quilt are symbols directly related to the Bakongo of Africa. These two symbols can also be found in the upper-left block of the Harriet Powers quilt in the collection of the Museum of Fine Arts, Boston (see fig. 118). (Collection of the author)

pick cotton. Law me, I don't know nothin' 'bout makin' quilts out of cotton till I comes to Texas.[29]

For the bottom layer, or lining, slaves used "anything they could get." This lining ranged from homespun to any combination of the fabrics used for the top portion of the quilt.

Slave narratives frequently refer to the fact that slaves learned how to use plant dyes expertly. Some dyes could be purchased in dry goods stores, while others grew naturally. Beech bark was used to achieve a slate color. Hickory bark and walnut bark colored fabric brown; cherry, elm, and red oak imparted red (a favorite color); cedar moss made yellow dye, while pine straw dyes yielded purple and wild indigo gave blue. Millie Evans of North Carolina remembered:

> To dye cloth brown we would take the cloth and put it in the water where leather had been tanned and let it soak, then set the color with apple vinegar. And we dyed blue with indigo and set the color with alum.[30]

Similarly, Jenny Procter of Alabama recalled that bits of cloth were sometimes dyed with sumac berries, sweet-gum berries, or poke berries. Additionally,

indigo, turkey red, and madder were available in the dry goods stores, and these or other dyes could have been purchased from drugstores.[31]

Slave preference for the color red in both their quilts and clothes has generated extensive speculation in historical literature. Among the many theories advanced for this preference, one concerns the climates of Africa and of the New World. It was speculated that the extremely high temperatures and humidity on both continents resulted in a preference for red because that color is more clearly visible in the hot sun. Another theory suggests that red is a strong color, hence most closely identified with "unbridled" or "primitive" emotions.

These theories fall wide of the mark. A more accurate interpretation relates to African survivals:

> The origins of the preference remain obscure but may have been African. So strongly did the West Africans enjoy red that among southern as well as Caribbean slaves the legend grew that it had betrayed them into slavery by laying them open to white deception. Red served as the royal color at Ardra, one of the great African centers of those religious rites which became voodoo in

60. Pieced linsey-woolsey quilt with wool ties. The backing is made with large squares of linsey-woolsey. This could well be another example of a quilt made by slaves for their own use (see also fig. 54). (The Valentine Museum, Richmond, Virginia)

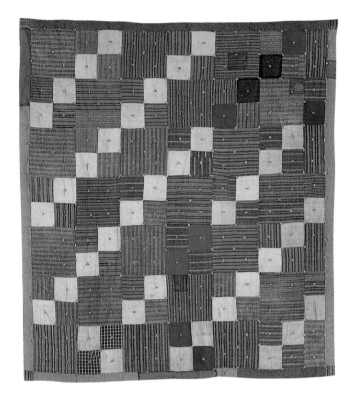

the New World, and it continued to serve similar purposes in the United States as well as Haiti. Theories vary, but the African attitude has plausibly been interpreted as an identification of red with life and fertility. As the color of blood it is made to represent the birth process for women and the roles of warrior and hunter for men.[32]

Additionally, red and white are the colors of Shango, a religious cult that originated in Nigeria among the Yoruba and has spread throughout the New World, including the United States. William Bascom notes:

> In Trinidad, as in northeastern Brazil, Shango is the name of the cult in which the Yoruba gods, known as "powers," are worshipped. Shango is the God of Thunder and Lightning and is identified with St. John the Baptist.... Shango's colors are red and white and his foods are sheep, cock, and rum.[33]

Patterns for the quilt pieces were yet another facet of the quilting process. The plantation mistress learned some traditional patterns from English copybooks. The extent to which these books influenced textile design in America in the eighteenth and nineteenth centuries has not been fully researched. Similarly unexplored is the influence of copybooks and their patterns, as transmitted by the mistress, to slave quilting in the antebellum South.

The term "copybook" appears in ex-slave testimony: "I learned to write in a copy book, and I'd write stories about Christ, and several different stories, I filled a great big copy book with practice."[34]

Slave women, however, learned traditional quilting patterns not only from the mistress but also from each other. The patterns mentioned most frequently in the WPA slave narratives include the following pre– and post–Civil War patterns:

1. Breakfast Dish
2. Sawtooth (silk)
3. Tulip Design (laid work)
4. "Prickle" Pear
5. Little Boy's Breeches
6. Birds All Over the Elements

61. Quilt from Mimosa Hall Plantation in Texas. When the Anglican bishop came each year to baptise, confirm, and perform marriages, the slaves made him a quilt—thus the reason for the chalices that form the design of this quilt. When the bishop left, the quilt was used by the children or the slaves. (The American Museum in Britain, Bath, England)

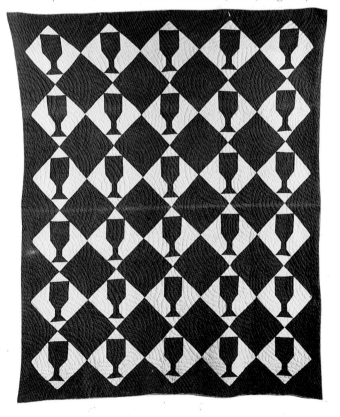

62, 63, 64, 65, 66, 67, 68, 69, 70. The master of slave Jennie Nevile Stroud returned eighteen quilts to her as a parting gift at the end of the Civil War. Thirteen of these quilts have survived and are owned by descendants, and they constitute the largest collection of quilts by a known slave quilter. Six of the quilts are illustrated here, together with a rag rug that she made and two embroidered-linen sewing bags that were used to carry needles, thread, and a thimble. Besides quilting, Jennie Stroud's skills included knitting, spinning, weaving, and embroidery. Tradition says that she was a beautiful woman who married and had eight children. (Collection of Mrs. Essie Leak, Chapel Hill, North Carolina)

7. Drunkard's Path
8. Railroad Crossing
9. Cocoanut Leaf ("That's laid work")
10. Cotton Leaf
11. Half an Orange
12. Tree of Paradise
13. Sunflower
14. Ocean Wave (silk)
15. Double Star
16. Swan's Nest
17. Log Cabin in the Lane
18. Lily in de Valley (silk)
19. Feathered Star
20. Fish Tail
21. Whirligig.[35]

The Nine Patch also appeared to have been a special favorite of slave quilters: "The Nine Patch pattern was a beauty, with little squares no bigger than your thumb nail."[36]

Slave women also used original patterns for their personal quilts. A former slave explained: "De quilts was warm and made from many pretty home-made

pattern."[37] Still another ex-slave commented: "She spends her time sitting in a wheel-chair sewing on quilts. She has several quilts that she has placed, some from very small scraps which she has cut without the use of any particular pattern."[38]

Certainly, some of the most ingenious original patterns were those which slaves adopted from their environment. Leaves were a particular favorite:

I want to show you a piece of work made entirely by a slave woman. Gal, bring me that quilt. Now you see the white linin' and the white between the blocks. My mother wove that white cloth an' the thread it's quilted with. The red an' green an' blue pieces was bought from the store, but she got the pattern by goin' out into the woods an' gettin a leaf to cut it by. The two parts of the pattern is cut from the bull-tongue leaf and the gopher grass. The quilt is about ninety years old, an' it was made when people was smart, an' went into the woods to get their patterns.[39]

Not all quilts were made out of old clothes and

46

63

64

65

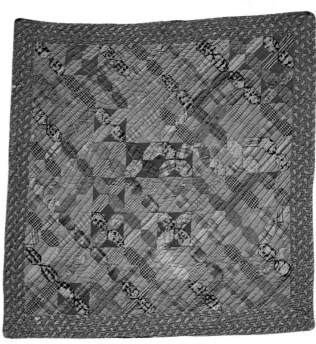

leftover plantation cloth. To purchase new cloth and trimmings, slaves earned extra income or "side money" by providing goods and services to the master and to neighboring plantation owners and town merchants. Foodstuffs offered for sale included produce from their own vegetable gardens, fresh eggs, poultry, fish, and wild game. Handmade goods included furniture, pottery, cane baskets, woven bottoms for chairs, quilts, counterpanes, and coverlets. One former slave explained: "My mother and father say de slaves made baskets and quilts and things and sell 'em for they-selves."[40]

Services rendered in exchange for money included midwifing and helping out on special occasions such as weddings. An ex-slave from Mississippi recalled assisting an "old maid daughter and two old maid sisters with their boarders." The slave was given a dollar for compensation. She recalled: "I thot I wuz rich; I tuk dat dollar an' bot me some calico an' made me sum quilts; I wuz so proud to have my own quilts an' pillows an' things."[41]

Slaves quilted during their "own time," which was usually at night, or Saturday afternoons and Sunday evenings. Inclement weather throughout the year also forced plantation owners to allow field hands to stay indoors. Free time included national holidays, such as Christmas and Thanksgiving, as well as regional celebrations and plantation festivities—log rollings, corn shuckings, candy pullings, etc. Often during more extended periods of free time, such as Sundays and

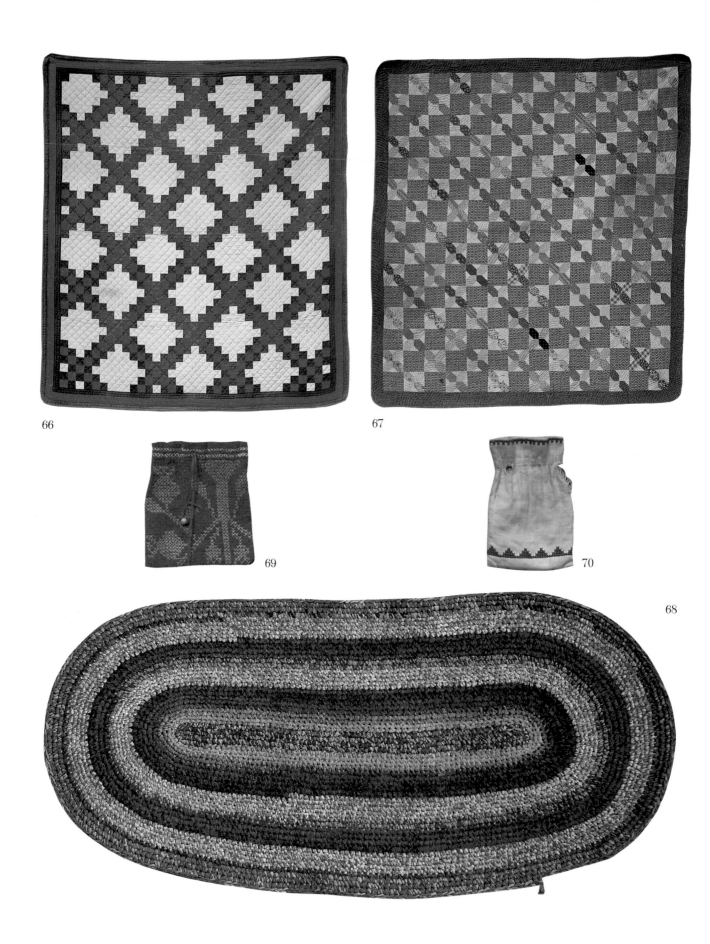

66

67

69

70

68

71. Pieced quilt made in a unique tulip pattern, c. 1850. (Collection of Mildred Gutrie, Snow Camp, North Carolina)

holidays, authorized quilting parties were held in the quarters for slave women to pass the time making quilts while telling stories and passing along gossip about plantation events.

Slaves were assigned day and evening tasks. Concerning the latter, one ex-slave stated: "De women folks has to spin four cuts of thread every night and make all de clothes. Some has to card cotton to make quilts and some weave and knits stockin's."[42]

House servants had the additional burden of staying late at night at the big house, and then having to complete their own chores on the quarters. These evenings were sometimes lightened, however, by telling jokes, stories, and engaging in plantation gossip. "Evenings we would spin on the old spinning wheel, quilt, make clothes, talk, tell jokes, and a few had learned to weave a little bit from Missus."[43]

Quilting in the quarters, however, was allowed only after all designated work assignments were completed, often well after sundown. In order to maximize the time required to work on their own projects, slaves came in from the fields or the big house and immediately began their own tasks. One slave recalled a childhood memory: "When I was a child at home we

72. Appliqué and embroidered floral quilt made by a slave in fine wool and left unfinished. It is inscribed "Frances M. Jolly 1839." (Smithsonian Institution, Washington, D.C.)

73. White muslin whole-cloth quilt made by slave Mary Williams and dated March 1848. Mary Williams was freed by the Document of Manumission on March 11, 1848, and the quilt is believed to have been made in celebration of her freedom. (Collection of Marguerite Doleman, Hagerstown, Maryland)

never had no time to play. When we came in from the cotton fields, we'd have to start quiltin."[44]

Another slave recalled: "I worked late and made pretty quilts."[45]

But quilting well into the night was not without hazard. A former slave recalled a very painful memory:

> My mammy she work in de fiel' all day and piece and quilt all night. Den she had to spin enough thread to make four cuts for de white fo'ks ebber night. Why sometime I nebber go to bed. Hab to hold de light for her to see by. She hab to piece quilts for de white folks too. Why dey is a scar on my arm yet where my brother let de pine drip on me. Rich pine war all de light we ebber hab. My brother was a holdin' de pine so's I can help mammy tack de quilt and he go to sleep and let it drop.[46]

Clearly, there were many tasks to be completed in a limited amount of time, and, as evidenced by the following testimony, everyone pitched in—men, women, and children; after all, there was some urgency. A new work day began at sunup!

> De women set by de fire piecin' quilts and spinnin' thread and de old men weave cotton baskets and chair bottoms and de young men work on de levees...[47]

In many instances, gender on slave plantations blurred. Slave women were involved in all phases of the plantation-growing economy—hoeing, hauling, chopping, and so forth. They could do expert carpentry, ironwork, and such.

For their part, men could sew, quilt, knit, crochet, embroider, and perform any other kind of needlework.

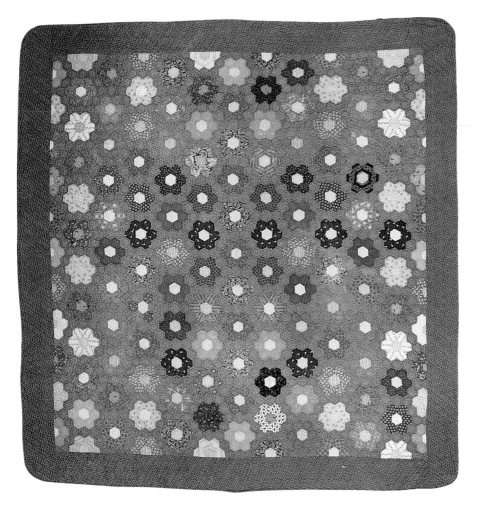

74. Pieced quilt, Grandmother's Flower Garden pattern, made on Watts Plantation near Laurens, South Carolina, prior to the Civil War. (The American Museum in Britain, Bath, England)

75. This Log Cabin quilt in the Streak o' Lightning design was made in Demopolis, Georgia, by Dolly Jackson, an "old slave," 1860–1870. Log Cabin quilts containing black fabric often served as signals on the Underground Railroad to identify "safe houses." (Louisiana State Museum, New Orleans, Louisiana)

According to Anne L. Macdonald in *No Idle Hands*, (pp. 23–24), men shared the responsibility for spinning, weaving, and knitting for the plantation household, and if they produced extra goods, could sell them outside. A male slave commented: "I used to could knit socks and I was jes'a li'l boy then, but I keep everything 'remembrance.'"[48]

"Lame Peter," Martha Washington's personal knitter, accompanied her to Mount Vernon as part of her dowry as a new bride (Macdonald, *No Idle Hands*, p. 24). Lame Peter apparently taught other slaves under Mrs. Washington's close tutelage and supervision. But when George Washington became president, he assumed responsibility for the household servants, and complained more than once about the inadequate quantity of stockings knit by "Lame Peter."

Emily P. Burke, a Northern white woman, observed the involvement of men at a quilting party and recorded her observations in her diary:

The slaves upon this plantation had their holidays and seasons for frolics as frequently as anyone could think was reasonable.... While I was on this plantation, the overseer's wife made a quilting at which she invited the field slaves, both men and women. It may seem strange to my readers to hear of men being invited to a quilting but I can say to them, that among the Southern field hands, the women can hoe as well as the men, and the men can sew as well as the women, and they engage in all departments of labor according to the necessity of the case without regard to sex. This quilting party was held in the night, the first part of which was devoted to work on the quilt, the latter part to festivity and dancing.[49]

According to oral testimonies obtained from descendants of former slaves, the male slaves simply watched and listened as mothers transmitted sewing skills and needle crafts to their daughters. They memorized what they heard and practiced what they saw. The mother's role in transmitting these skills is

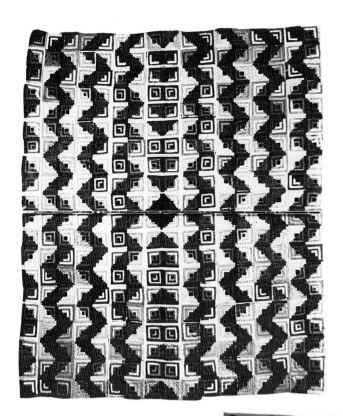

clearly reflected by the comment of an ex-slave from Arkansas: "Mama learned me to knit and I used to crochet a lot. She sure learned me to work and I ain't sorry."[50]

Children were often involved at an early age in the quilting process: they put filling in the quilts; they threaded the needles; they held the light. "I been knitting socks and sewing and piecing quilts ever since I was eight years old."[51] And another slave commented, "'Bout the only work I ever done was help watch the geese and turkeys and fill the quilts."[52]

Historians have reported the various goods the master provided for his slaves. But they seldom, if ever, mention quilts that the masters gave their slaves either routinely or as a gift or prize for special achievement.

Routine yearly allotments did include quilts. It is interesting that sexism played a role even in the distribution of slave goods. One slave said: "The ex-slave doesn't remember any feathers in the covering for his pallet in the corner of his cabin, but says that Mr. Campbell always provided the slaves with blankets

76. Appliqué quilt top with embroidered date "March 19, 1852." A note attached to the quilt states: "This quilt was made on the William Dean Plantation in New Orleans, before the Civil War, by one of Mrs. Catherine Dean's slaves whom they called 'Yellow Bill.' He sewed every inch with his own hand." The 1850 census lists a "William Dean" as residing in the city of New Orleans, New Orleans Parish. It is unclear from the listing whether Dean's residence was a plantation, a farm, or a mansion. The central panel contains four floral cutouts that scholars believe were intended to be snake symbols. The snake plays a major role in African mythology, and throughout the diaspora. The snake was considered to be a source of life, a symbol of fertility and of the rainbow, and it was also believed to be an intermediary with ancestors. It is known that slaves sometimes put snake symbols on their clothes. (Collection of the author)

77. Pieced quilt embroidered with a variety of plants that was made by a slave boy, approximately sixteen years old, on a North Carolina plantation, c. 1860. Most of the wool blocks show plants characteristic of the young slave's locale, such as those used for making plant dyes and bed ticking. (Collection of the author)

78. Crocheted tablecloth made by a slave of Dr. Josiah Ellegood in Delaware before 1865. Photograph by Doyce Croy. (Stephens County Historical Museum, Duncan, Oklahoma)

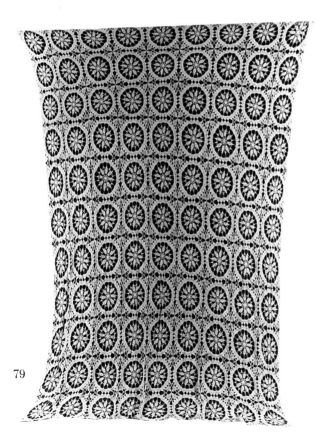

79

80

79. Crocheted bedspread, c. 1840, made by Phyllis, a slave and the great-great-grandmother of Alphonso Biggs, who owns six of her quilts and two of her crocheted bedspreads. (Collection of Alphonso Biggs, Columbus, Georgia)

80. Crocheted bedspread made by Phyllis, a slave who also made the spread illustrated in figure 79 and the quilts illustrated in figures 109–114. (Collection of Alphonso Biggs, Columbus, Georgia)

81. White candlewick spread, c. 1840. (Collection of Mrs. Mattye Reed, Greensboro, North Carolina)

81a. Detail of the center motif in the candlewick spread illustrated in figure 81. (Collection of Mrs. Mattye Reed, Greensboro, North Carolina)

81a
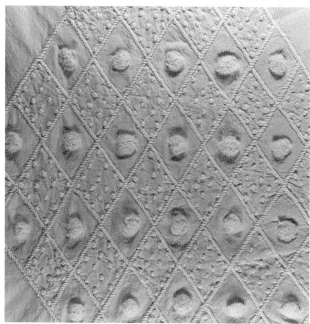

55

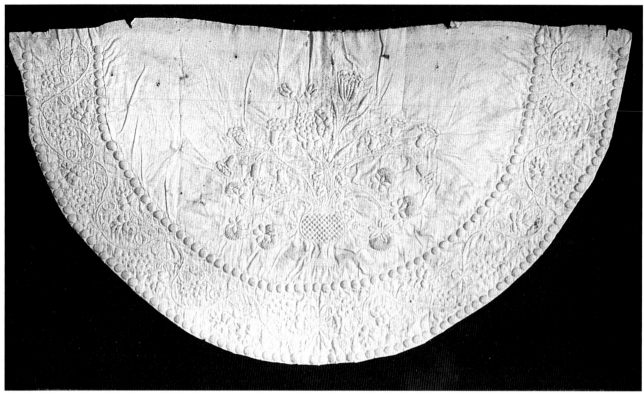

82. This handsome white cover for a dressing table is decorated with elegant stuffed work showing a vase of flowers framed by a serpentine grapevine. It was made by slaves around 1815. (Charleston Museum, Charleston, South Carolina)

83. Rag rug in blue, pink, and white, 1850–1860. The rug was made by slaves on a loom in Guilford County, North Carolina. (Collection of Mrs. Mattye Reed, Greensboro, North Carolina).

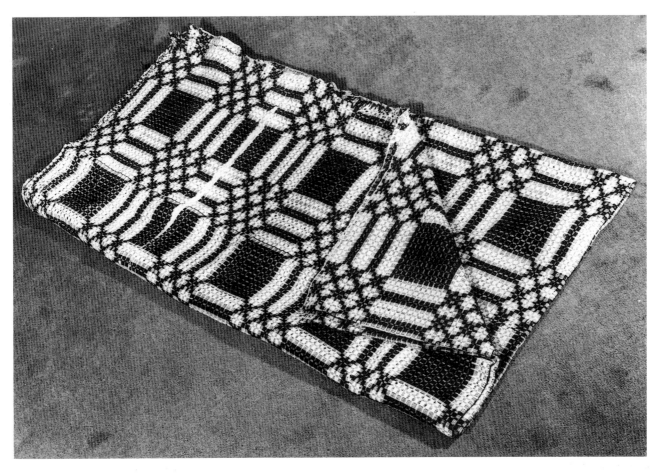

84. Woven coverlet made by slaves, c. 1845. (San Antonio Museum Association, San Antonio, Texas)

85. Woven wool coverlet, slave-made, c. 1863. (Alabama Department of Archives and History, Montgomery, Alabama)

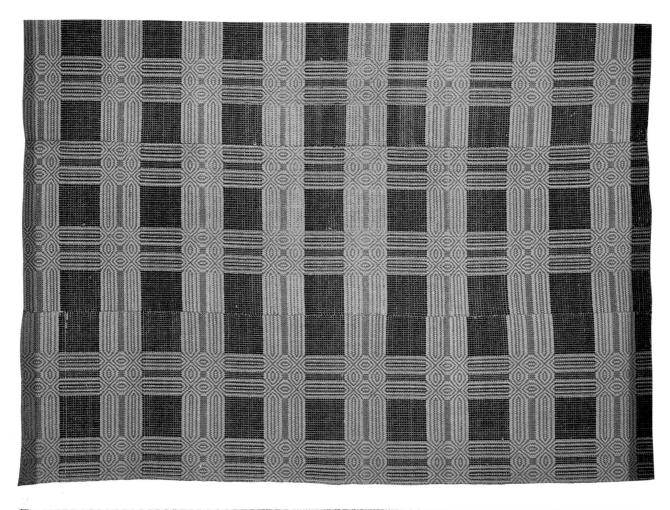

86. Woven wool coverlet said to have been made by a slave woman in Rockingham County, North Carolina. (The Museum of the Confederacy, Richmond, Virginia)

87. Wool coverlet probably woven by a female slave on the Nelson Clayton Plantation in Lee County, Alabama, during the Civil War. (The Museum of the Confederacy, Richmond, Virginia)

88. Wool coverlet woven on a Jacquard loom possibly in Tuscaloosa County, Alabama, c. 1840. (Old Tavern Museum, Tuscaloosa, Alabama)

and the women with quilts."[53] An additional comment came from an ex-slave who said: "We took old gunny sacks and put leaves in dem to make a bed and we slept on de floor and had a old spread and de white folks gave us some old quilts."[54]

Sometimes quilts were offered as a prize for the best performance in a specified activity. The following experience is an example:

> Frolics were often given on the Harper plantation. They usually consisted of dancing and banjo playing. Slaves from other plantations sometimes attended, but it was necessary to secure a pass from their master and mistress in order to do so. A prize was given to the person who would "buck dance" the steadiest with a tumbler of water balanced on the head. A cake or a quilt was often given as the prize.[55]

89, 90, 91. Three wool coverlets handwoven in Northport, Alabama, by Aunt Tish Prewitt, a slave of Mrs. Elizabeth Prewitt. (Old Tavern Museum, Tuscaloosa, Alabama)

The comment of another slave was: "When the war was done he come and got me and we went to Barton County, Georgia. When I left they give me my feather bed, two good coverlets and my clothes. White folks hated fo me to leave."[56]

90

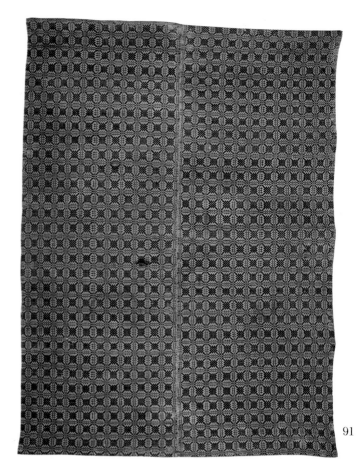

91

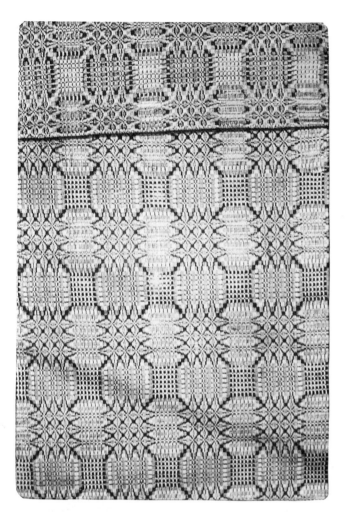

Certainly, slave women were both talented and versatile. A large number of WPA interviewees detailed many skills related to textile production. The list included sewing, knitting, crocheting, quilting, expert mending, embroidery, tatting, spinning, and weaving. One ex-slave proudly reported: "I can't cut out no dress and make it, but I can use a needle on patching and quilting. Can't nobody beat me doin' that. I can knit, too. I can make stockings, gloves, and all such things."[57]

Garments such as children's stockings, mittens, scarves, and caps were knitted by slave women in their spare time. One slave woman who knitted every available moment was described later by her son, who recalled that "she would go about with her knitting in her pockets, and if she had to walk from the cabin to the house she would always knit wherever she walked to. Sometimes she would sit on top of the mule on her way to the field knitting."[58]

92. Detail of a handwoven wool coverlet in the Gentleman's Fancy pattern. It was made by Mahala Clarke Knight's slave at Laurel Hill Plantation, Virginia. (Old Slave Mart, Charleston, South Carolina)

93. Detail of a handwoven wool coverlet made by a slave near La Grange, Georgia. (Old Slave Mart, Charleston, South Carolina)

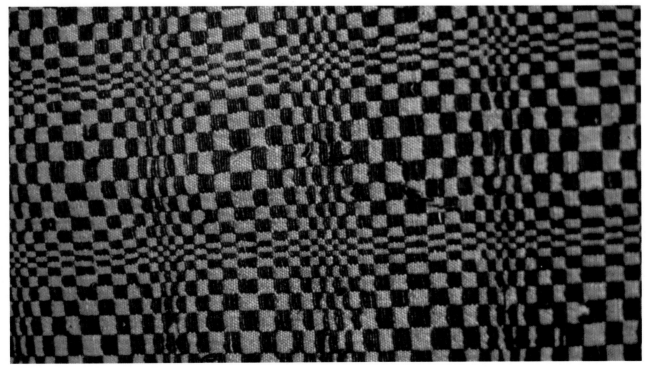

94. Loom house used by slaves at Melrose Plantation, Melrose, Louisiana.

95. Interior of the loom house at Melrose Plantation (fig. 94) showing the looms used by slaves.

96. Handwoven and embroidered counterpane made by Sarah May, a sixteen-year-old slave girl, around 1824 in Charleston, South Carolina, from thread spun on the plantation. (Collection of American Life and Culture, Dallas, Texas)

A "champion knitter" is how another African American recalled her slave mother: "My mother was the knittin'est woman ever seed in my life. She could be like settin' here in dis room knittin' and you be out de door outside de house and you could hear dem knittin' needles poppin' same as somebody was in here poppin' corn."[59]

Slaves often created their own knitting needles, using twigs or two pieces of straw. They also managed to improvise yarn with ravelings from cloth produce bags such as feed, flour, and tobacco sacks.

Leonard Stavisky, in *The Negro Artisan in the South Atlantic States, 1800–1860*, added additional categories: "Almost every woman was familiar with the usual domestic skills. Sewing, pleating, washing, starching, ironing, cooking, knitting, and weaving were minimum essentials."[60]

The glue that helped cement the fragile and uncertain existence of slave life was their oral lore. It was an ever-present force—sometimes the main event, as in the slave quilting party—and sometimes the background event while slaves sewed, mended, knitted, and such. But present it was. While the official learning of the master's literate world was denied the slave, it was the slave's oral lore that taught moral lessons, values, attitudes, strategies for survival, rites of passage, and humor!

Folklore helped to preserve the slaves' sense of identity, of knowing who they were and how they perceived the world. Folk traditions also served as a buffer between the slaves and a hostile world, both on and off the plantation. For it was in the slave quarters that African traditions first met and intersected with Euro-American cultural forms. What emerged were

97. Slave-made counterpane, c. 1800. (Alabama Department of Archives and History, Montgomery, Alabama)

transformations, adaptations, and reinterpretations.

Any gathering in the quarter for quilting or for a frolic "provided the means to build community through shared ritual."[61] The group life in the quarters was the slave equivalent of group life in Africa.

It was in the group that slaves learned of births, deaths, illnesses, social events, and secret meetings. And, most important, slaves in the quarters learned from house servants what was going on in the big house. Their language was coded:[62]

EXPRESSION	MEANING
Ary	Any
Big Hat	Conceited Negro
Bush Arbors	Secret churches built out of arbors
Bush Whacker	Confederate Soldiers
Burial Box	Slave Coffin
Bugs in de wheat	Look out for Patrollers
Break down	Slave dance
Cross You	To whip a slave by cutting his back into squares with a whip
Cooling board	Board on which dead slaves were placed
Church courtin'	Couples leave church to court while services are going on
Confuddle	Confuse
Cornstack Preacher	Slave preacher who presided over secret meetings
Comboodle	Everything (that takes place in whole comboodle)

Quilts were used to send messages. On the underground railroad, those with the color black in them were hung on the line to indicate a place of refuge (safe house). Other effects were achieved with clothes. During the Civil War, clothes hanging on the line in a certain way meant that troop movement would be in that direction. Triangles in quilt design signified prayer messages or a prayer badge, a way of offering prayer.

Colors were very important to slave quilt makers. The color black indicated that someone might die. A blue color was believed to protect the maker.

Various beliefs and superstitions were related to quilt making. For example, it was considered bad luck to begin any activity on Friday that could not be finished on that day, because:

Glad you come out here but sorry of de day, 'cause it is a Friday and all de jay-birds go to see de devil dat day of de week. It's a bad day to begin a garment, or quilt or start de lye hopper or 'simmon beerkeg or just anything important to yourself on dat day. Dere is just one good Friday in de year and de others is given over to de devil, his imps, and de jay-birds. Does I believe all dat? I believes it 'nough not patch dese old breeches 'til tomorrow and not start my 'simmon beer, when de frost fall on them dis fall, on a Friday.[63]

Another slave reinforced this belief: "Don't start to sew a piece of goods on Friday unless you are sure you can get it done before night for that is bad luck."[64]

It was also considered bad luck to make certain types of quilts such as lay quilts or "laid work" (appliqué). How much of this applied to their personal quilt making remains a conjecture. However, many of the quilts that have survived are appliquéd.

98. Slave-made counterpane, c. 1845. (Alabama Department of Archives and History, Montgomery, Alabama)

I Sell the Shadow to Support the Substance.

SOJOURNER TRUTH.

99. An 1864 albumen silver print of Sojourner Truth with her knitting. An orator and abolitionist, Sojourner Truth was a former slave who won great fame in the Civil War period. (The National Portrait Gallery, Smithsonian Institution, Washington, D.C.)

100. A hand-printed photograph of Harriet Tubman in her middle years. Harriet Tubman (1820?–1913), an abolitionist, was born a slave in Dorchester County, Maryland, about 1820. In 1849 she escaped from her master and went to the North with the aid of the Underground Railroad. During the years 1849–1859 Tubman became famous as the "Moses of her people," for through her resourcefulness, intelligence, and determination she brought more than three hundred slaves to the North on the Underground Railroad. (Courtesy J. B. Leib Photo Co., York, Pennsylvania)

Blood on quilts was a sign of bad luck. Throwing a quilt over the roof would ensure good luck: "All de neighbors comed to de quiltin's, and when de quilts was finished, dey throwed it over de head of de house. Dat brung good luck."[65]

It was considered bad luck to make a perfect quilt or to use straight, unbroken lines. This attitude reflects the folk belief of plantation slaves that evil spirits follow straight lines, and also that an imperfect quilt would distract the devil in the night.

Slaves valued "good talk," and the subject of this talk was Jack-a-ma-lantern, Raw Head and Bloody Bones, witches, ghosts, "Old Scratch," the devil; trickster tales such as "Old Master and John"; and personal experience narratives about the slave experience (such as an unsettling exchange with the patrollers).

Traditional folk tales were passed off as first-person experience in narratives:

Now I'll tell you another incident. This was in slave times. My mother was a great hand for nice quilts. There was a white lady had died and they were goin' to have a sale. Now this is true stuff. They had the sale and mother went

67

101. An oil portrait of Harriet Tub-man in old age wearing a hand-knitted shawl. (The National Por-trait Gallery, Smithsonian Institu-tion, Washington, D.C.)

and bouth two quilts. And let me tell you, we couldn't sleep under 'em. What happened? Well, they'd pinch your toes till you couldn't stand it. I was just a boy and I was sleepin' with my mother when it happened. Now that's straight stuff. What do I think was the cause? Well, I think that white lady didn't want no nigger to have them quilts. I don't know what mother did with 'em, but that white lady just wouldn't let her have 'em.[66]

They talked about astrological phenomena, such as the dark day of May 19, 1780. "Den one day de sun turned black and de chickens went to roost in de day time."[67] And slaves told and retold the day the stars fell, complete with sounds and gestures: this occurrence was a favorite one in the repertory of Mattie Dillworth, an ex-slave:

Mattie lies all day in a poor bed of old quilts

and pillows, but when she tries to tell about the stars falling, which she does over and over, she sits up in bed and illustrates with her long, bony, black hands how the "star cum, an' kep' on cummin'" and as she tries to reproduce her remembrance of the sound which sounded to her like "cr-e-e-k, plumpfh" her withered lips curl and stretch over her toothless gums in the effort.[68]

Proverbs were transmitted from one slave to another: "Old sheep knows de way—little lambs gotta learn it"; "bird can't fly so high that he don't have to come to the ground to eat"; "old cow needs her tail more than once to shoo flies"; "never let the same bee sting you twice."

The plantation quilting party was the occasion that allows us to view slave folklore as a "social event, a ritual, an expression of community,"[69] and as theater.

THE QUILTING PARTY

Well, yes, they used to have lots of nice parties. We would have quilting parties, and we'd put three or four quilts in the frame on top of one another; and then they would put the frame way up high; then while they were quilting each quilt they would sing and have lots of fun. I remember they used have a little song, but I can't remember but one line of it to save my life,—went something like this—les see, "Jim crack corn and I don't care...."[1]

The "quilting" is the slave term for this type of traditional all-female party, which has become generally known as a quilting bee. The WPA slave narrative materials indicate that quiltings were fun-filled, freewheeling affairs organized by women but also attended by men and children. Entertainment included the mandatory sewing, but there was also eating, drinking, storytelling, game playing, gossiping, singing, dancing, and even courting. An ex-slave from Kentucky described her experiences:

I remember wen we uster hav big time quilting on dem days we sho had a big time fore we start in de morning wid a water melon feast, den weums quilt while a big dinner war spread out den after dinner we'd quilt in de evening den supper and a big dance dat night,

wid de banjo a humming en us niggers a dancing, "Oh, Lawdy wat good days dem war."[2]

And because quiltings were freewheeling, arguments and fistfights and shootings were not uncommon:

I 'member one night dey had a quiltin' in de quarters. De quilt was up in de frame, an' day wah all jes' quiltin' an' singin', "All God's Chilluns are a Gatherin' Home," w'en a drunk man wannid to preach, an' he jumped up on de quilt! Hit all fell down on de flo', an' dey all got fightin' mad at 'im. Dey locked 'im in de smokehouse 'til mornin', but dey diden nobody tell Mistus nuffin 'bout it.[3]

102. Nineteenth-century handmade wooden quilting frame from Shelby, North Carolina. This type of frame was used on ante-bellum plantations by both whites and slaves and would have been suspended from the rafters when not in use. (Private collection)

102a. Detail showing the tongue-and-groove construction of the quilting frame in figure 102. (Private collection)

103. Flatirons like these were used by slaves as a weight to hold quilting materials secure when no quilting frame was available.

In the WPA narratives, slaves described all types of work-related celebrations: cotton pickings, finger pickings (where seeds were picked off the cotton by hand), corn shuckings, corn shellings, house coverings, logrollings, candy pullings, cording and spinning bees, and, of course, the quilting parties. Of these, corn shuckings, a male celebration, and female-organized quiltings were mentioned most frequently. On some plantations, these two were held the same evening with the men holding forth at the corn shucking and the women at the quilting.

For the most part, slaves remembered all of these events with some fondness. But quilting parties held a very special place in their memory:

> De marsters, dey planned de cornshuckin's, and cotton pickin's, and logrollin's and pervided de eats and liquor. But de quiltin' parties b'longed to de slaves. Dey 'ranged 'em deir own selfs and done deir own 'vitin' and fixed up deir own eats, but most of de marsters would let 'em have a little sompin' extra lak brown sugar or 'lasses and some liquor.[4]

Two powerful forces helped establish the quiltings as an important part of African-American plantation life: the need for a social outlet, and the need for warm bed coverings. By the nineteenth century, slaves were generally given commercial blankets every third year. Quilts and other types of handmade bed coverings helped compensate for such meager supplies.

On the plantation, there were basically two types of slave quilting parties: elaborate affairs in which each phase of the events was orchestrated, and more impromptu scaled-down affairs that rotated nightly from cabin to cabin.

The elaborate parties usually occurred on special occasions such as Christmas and at the end of the harvest season. Central to this type of party was the quilting manager, whose normal plantation role was that of wet nurse, cook, or seamstress.

It was the quilting manager's job to get elderly slaves who could no longer work in the fields to piece the quilt tops prior to the quilting party. She also arranged for supplies, food, and entertainment.

Normally, four people worked on a quilt, one at each corner. The first team to finish a quilt received a prize. This kind of organization meant that three to twelve quilts could be completed during the course of an evening. A Georgia slave recalled:

> At quiltin' bees, four folks wuz put at every quilt, one at every corner. Dese quilts had been pieced by old slaves who warn't able to work in de field. Quiltings always tuk place durin' de winter when dere warn't much to do. A prize wuz always give to de four which finished dere quilt fust. 'Freshments went 'long wid dis too.[5]

Occasionally, masters on some of the larger plantations, who were eager to impress their neighbors with evidence of wealth and importance, helped to stage elaborate quilting parties. These parties offered several advantages for the slave: time off, more elaborate party fare, and entertainment. An ex-slave from Florida remembered:

> Much work was needed to supply the demands of so large a plantation but the slaves were given time off for frolics [dances, quilting, weddings]. These gatherings were attended by old and young from neighboring plantations. There was always plenty of food, masters vying with one another for the honor of giving his slaves the finest parties.
>
> There was dancing and music. On the Folson Plantation, Bryant, the youngest of the masters, furnished the music. He played the fiddle and liked to see the slaves dance "cutting the pigeon wing."[6]

Master-sponsored quilting parties were often held at Christmastime, especially on Christmas Day. A Texas slave recalled: "We had a big quilting Christmas day. We'd piece de quilts outta scraps. Some couldn' quilt. Dey'd dance in the yard all day."[7]

Recorded nineteenth-century historical documents verify that slave quilting parties were very much a part of the plantation scene. Theological students at the Lutheran Seminary in Lexington, South Carolina, were required to keep a journal and read aloud from it at synod meetings. Thadeus Street Boinest, a student at the seminary, recorded the following entry in his diary: "Friday, December 24 (1847)...Mr. R[auch] bro W[arner] & myself went up to old Mr. Rauch's patrolling, as there was a negro quilting there, we had some good sport and went home to Mr. R[auch]'s about 1 oclk."[8] One can only imagine what "good sport" meant, but it seems fairly certain that these particular patrollers were intent on having fun at the expense of the slaves attending the quilting party.

The master's generosity may have been related to productivity at harvest time. Activities like quiltings and corn shuckings were promised as a reward for finishing work on time. One former slave recalled:

> My mother went to cornshuckings, cotton pickings, and quiltings. They must have had wonderful times, to hear her tell it. She said

104. Appliqué quilt, possibly made by slaves, that orginally belonged to the Robertson family, one of the earliest and best-known families of Tennessee. (Tennessee State Museum, Nashville, Tennesse)

105. Quilt made for the Wade family in Rutherford, Tennessee, c. 1840. (Old Courthouse Museum, Vicksburg, Mississippi)

106. Star quilt, c. 1850, made in Lebanon, Tennessee, by a slave owned by Mrs. Jane Greer Jackson. "Jane G. Jackson" is stamped in very faded ink on each of the four borders. (San Antonio Museum Association, San Antonio, Texas)

107. Pieced quilt, Whig's Defeat pattern, made by an unknown slave, c. 1850. (Vann House, Atlanta, Georgia)

that after the corn was shucked, cotton picked, or quilts quilted, they always gave them plenty of good things to eat and drink and let them loose to enjoy themselves for the balance of the night. Those things took place at harvest time, and everyone looked forward to having a good time at that season. Mother said that Marse John was particular with his slaves, and wouldn't let them go just anywhere to these things.[9]

Winter evening quilting parties held in specific cabins on a rotating basis were a staple of the slave community. Tradition and ritual were very much a part of these activities. In fact, the evening's festivities always began with a traditional response: "Dey'd say 'I's gon'a step over to one or another's cabin'—en word ud git aroun' en 'for you knowd it dey'd be a crowd. We allus said 'Just step over' no matter how far it wuz."[10]

A Georgia slave recalled:

One of the most enjoyable affairs in those days was the quilting party. Every night they would assemble at some particular house and help that person finish her quilts. The next night, a visit would be made to someone else's home and so on, until everyone had a sufficient amount of bed-clothing made for the winter. Besides, this was an excellent chance to get together for a pleasant time and discuss the latest gossip.[11]

The "round robin" quilting parties were further discussed by another Georgia slave:

Every one would go together to a different person's house on each separate night of the week and finish that person's quilts. Each night this was repeated until everyone had a sufficient amount of covering for the winter. Any slave from another plantation desiring to attend these frolics could do so after securing a pass from their master.[12]

Another version of this type of quilting was held on Saturday afternoon. While the male slaves went fishing, the women met at a preselected site to help with each other's quilts.

74

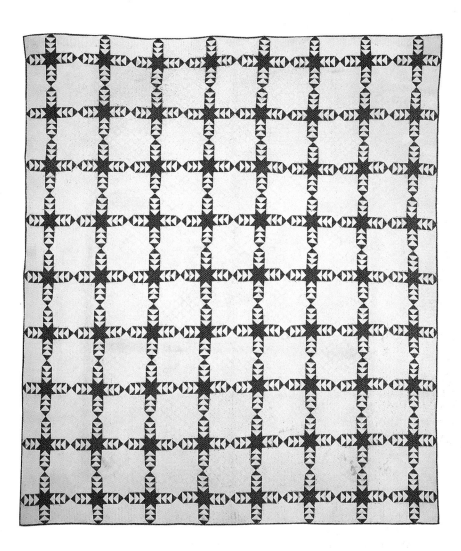

108. Pieced quilt, Wild Geese Flying pattern, c. 1847. The back is made of white homespun cotton. The inscription "M. Hamilton, July 1847" is embroidered in tiny cross-stitch in one corner. (San Antonio Museum Association, San Antonio, Texas)

Sometimes special circumstances determined where the evening party would be held, like helping a single male parent who was attempting to raise children alone. A South Carolina slave remembered: "One time dey give my daddy a quilting and ax several women to come dere. Dey had a lot of chillun to cover up.... Mistress tell dem to give the women [who come] scraps from de loom house."[13]

Most slaves agreed that the master's permission was generally sought to give a quilting party. On many plantations, such permission appears to have been routine. Occasionally, there was a proviso. As one ex-slave stated: "You would have to git permission from the old mass'r to have a good time like that. He would say, 'I don't want no fussing or no shooting.'"[14]

But knowing the location of an event is a far cry from really knowing what goes on at that event. Some masters routinely checked on the "activities" in the quarters. One Arkansas slave remembered: "The master would go there, too, and look at them and see what they were doing and how they were doing....They would do that at the candy pullin' too, and anything else."[15]

It can be fairly certain that the shared ritual, the exchange of information, the storytelling, the gossiping, and even the singing and dancing were carried on out of the master's sight. To ensure secrecy, the slaves would "turn a pot upside down right in front of the door. They said that would keep the sound from going outside."[16] This practice probably had African origins, and the slaves' belief in its effectiveness doubtless gave them confidence to enjoy themselves and to make noise in the process.

There is a definite correlation between the regularity of the quilting parties and the ample supply of bedding that slaves reported in their oral testimony. According

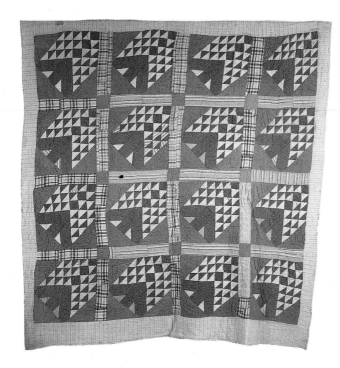

109, 110, 111, 112, 113, 114. Pieced quilts made by Phyllis, a slave imported from the Congo in 1818 as a twelve- or thirteen-year-old girl. She became the plantation cook, but she also showed considerable craft skills, as well as being able to do carpentry and blacksmithing. (Collection of Alphonso Biggs, Columbus, Georgia)

to a Georgia slave: "Us did have plenty of Kivver dough. Folkes was all time a-piecin quilts and having quiltin's. All dat sort of wuk was done at night."[17]

Food for the quiltings was provided in several ways: the master gave extra supplies; the slaves provided the fare out of their own provisions and gardens; or food was provided by the master without his knowledge or permission. As one ex-slave explained:

> De womans what was cooks at de big house tied sacks 'round deir waists under deir skirts, and all thoo' de day dey would drap a little of dis, and some of dat, in de sacks. When dey poured it out at night, dere was plenty of good somepin' t'eat.[18]

But whatever the source, the quilting supper, by all accounts, was both varied and plentiful. Meats ranged from freshly barbecued hog to chitterlings to chicken; depending on availability, wild game, which was trapped and killed, often included ducks, geese, squirrels, rabbits, possum, pigeons, dove, partridge, and deer.

Added to this fare were such staples as collard greens and cornpone. Dessert selections included pound cakes, ginger cake, apple pies, and peach pies.

110

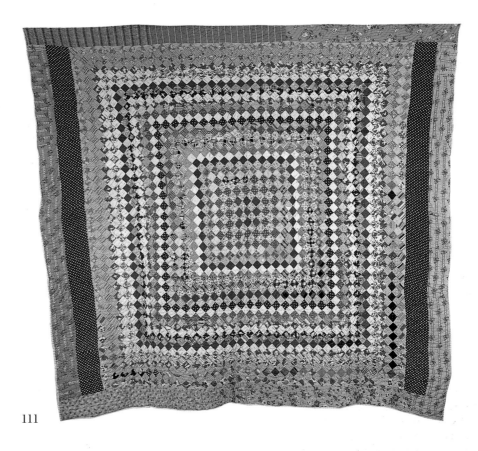

111

Beverages included cider, whiskey, persimmon beer, or freshly brewed coffee. A Georgia slave said:

> Quiltin's wuz a heap of fun. Sometimes two or three famlies had a quiltin' together. Folkses would quilt some un' den dey passed 'round de toddy. Some would be cookin' while de others wuz a quiltin' an' den when supper wuz ready dey all stopped to eat. Dem colla'd greens wi'd cornpone an' plenty of ginger cakes an fruit puffs an' big old pots of coffee wuz mighty fine eatin' to us den.[19]

The entertainment portion of the slave quilting consisted of singing, dancing, listening to music, and playing traditional games.

After the quilting, the cabins were cleared of furnishings and the dancing began. Sometimes the dancing took place in the yard of the cabin, or masters gave permission for the dance to be held in dependency buildings, such as the kitchen.

A North Carolina slave remembered a favorite aunt who was well known in the community as a talented dancer: "One of the slaves, my aint, she wuz a royal slave. She could dance all over de place wid a tumbler of water on her head, widout spilling it. She sho could tote herself. I always luved to see her come to Church. She sho could tote herself."[20]

The musical instruments that accompanied the dancers came from the African-American musical tradition. They include "blow guills," bones that were knocked together, and fiddles, which were gourds made with horsehair strings.

Slaves played traditional games such as "thimble" and "spin the plate." Concerning the latter game, one ex-slave recalled:

> Oh, dey have dem quiltin at night and would play en go on in the kitchen. Turn plate en different little things like dat. I don' know how dey do it but I remembers I hear dem talkin somethin bout "turnin plate." Wasn' big enough to explain nothin bout what dey meant. I just knows dey would do dat en try to make some kind of motion like.[21]

A very important but overlooked aspect of the quilting parties were the courtship games. Two such courtship games (both involving kissing) appeared to be fairly common: In the first, a boy attempted to throw a quilt over one of the girls and catch her, so he could claim his reward of a hug and a kiss (a game also known in the white tradition and fairly commonly reported in nineteenth-century diaries and memoirs); in the second version of this game, the slave women selected the most handsome male at the party, draped

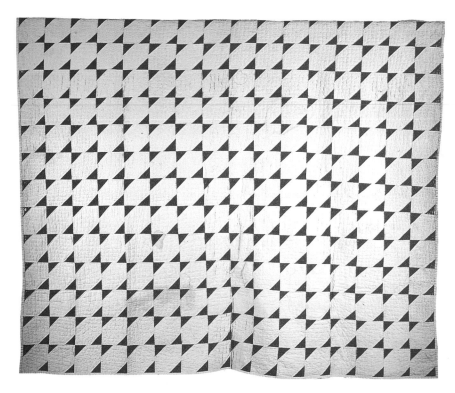

112

a quilt around him (rendering him immobile), and *all* the women were entitled to a kiss.

Another aspect of courtship involved the use of ritualized language with traditional responses. The meaning was understood by both parties. A male slave described the process:

> How did I court the girls? Me, I didn't court them. I didn't court them a' tall. All of them loved me; I didn't [need to] court.... They would call one another "Hon," and I would say, "Sweet." And they would say, "Let's go home," and there would be something going on like a quilting, and I would go and take a gal home.[22]

Traditional modes of behavior and responses are further reflected in the following account of courtship ritual at a quilting party attended by a slave and Choctaw Indian women. Of particular interest is how the simple juxtaposition of chairs revealed meaning and expectation:

> While all were busily engaged quilting, a young brave, Martin Whistler, appeared upon the scene bearing a number of squirrels which he had killed and presented them to Betsy [a comely young Indian maid] for preparation for the noon meal. He took a chair near the object of his affections and would occasion-ally reach out and tap her on the shoulder. She would smilingly insist that he quit and in a coy manner pretend to draw away from his reach. To show that the attention paid her by the admiring youth was not unwelcome, she would soon have her chair scooted over to within reaching distance so that the gentle tapping would be repeated. This continued until late evening when the quilting was finished and the party, which was composed of both colored and Indian women, departed for their several homes. Of course, the young man found it to be convenient to go in the same direction, and at the same time, as the charmer of his life and, "lawsee de next mawnin we heead dey was mahied up."[23]

The finale to this story may be somewhat misleading, because even though the two races demonstrated a close neighborliness, they rarely intermarried.

Male slaves frequently offered small gifts—a spool of thread or a thimble—as tokens of affection or to indicate their interest in a woman. In referring to his father, one slave explains:

> Mother never had much to say, and the other girls would have a big time talking. He noticed that she was sewing with ravelings and he said, "Lady, next time I come I'll bring

you a spool of thread if you don't mind." He brought the thread and she didn't mind, and from then on, they went to courting. Finally they married. They married very shortly after the War.[24]

Accompanying the courtship rituals were traditional riddling and ring plays. The latter involved a great deal of movement, but were not considered dancing because "one did not cross one's feet."

Each game consisted of a moving ring that circled about one or two central participants. Those in the circling ring usually clapped their hands while singing a song that provided the story being enacted, or played, by the participants in the center. For instance, a woman in the middle, designated as "Miss Susie Anna Brown," would play according to the following:

> Go round and round the circle
> Miss Susie Anna Brown (repeat)
> Now steady in the circle
> Miss Susie Anna Brown
> Go wipe dem di'mon winders
> Miss Susie Anna Brown
> Now let me see your motion

> Miss Susie Anna Brown
> 'Tis a mighty pretty motion
> Miss Susie Anna Brown

Each verse encouraged a progression in the play, and the relation of the surrounding ring to the central participant corresponded to that of counterpoint and theme, where the one accentuates and complements the other. With the first verse, "Miss Brown" would be chosen and would take her place in the ring; during the second, Miss Brown would prepare her performance; in the third, she would begin a wiping motion with her arms as if she were washing windows, while the hands of the others would be joined and raised to represent the windows; the fourth and fifth verses would be sung as encouragement; then a new figure would take the center and the play would begin again.[25]

No matter the type of quilting event, there was never any doubt about who planned the quiltings, with their food, games, and dancing. Women were in firm control. As one male ex-slave from Georgia said when asked by a WPA interviewer about plantation quilting parties: "Now lady, what would a old Nigger man

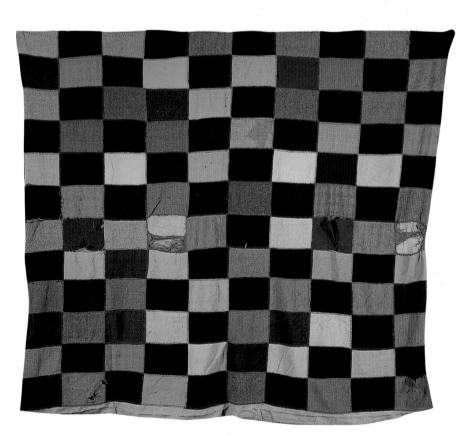

113

114

know 'bout somepin' dat didn't nothin' but womans have nothin' to do wid?"[26]

Men were invited, but only at a point in the festivities when slave women allowed them to come—occasionally after the quilting, and sometimes after the food! A Georgia ex-slave stated, "Dey went f'um one plantation to another to quiltin's. Atter de womans got thou' quilting and et a big dinner, den dey axed de mens to come in and dance wid 'em."[27]

It would appear that men were bit players as opposed to central characters. They threaded the needles; they held the light (often tallow candles); they provided an escort service home (if asked); they were dancing partners; they kept the fire going; and, generally, they played the musical instruments that accompanied the dancing.

An Arkansas slave explained, "At the quilting, they'd [the women] get down and quilt. The boys and young men would be there too and they would thread the needles and laugh and talk with girls, and the women would gossip."[28]

But minor role aside, slave testimony suggests that men enjoyed themselves thoroughly at the quiltings. As one ex-slave stated succinctly: "Mens had good time at the quiltin's too."[29]

So sure were masters that male slaves would attend a quilting party in spite of risks and dangers to personal safety that at least on one occasion, "the quilting" was used as a bait to trap a rebellious slave. The plan backfired, according to the following account given by a Texas ex-slave:

My pappy wasn't 'fraid of nothin'. He am light cullud from de white blood, and he runs away sev'ral times. Dere am big woods all round and we sees lots of run-awayers. One old fellow name John been a run-awayer for four years and de patterrollers tries all dey tricks, but dey can't cotch him. Dey wants him bad, 'cause it 'spire other slaves to run away if he stays a-loose. Dey sote de trap for him. Dey knows he like good eats, so dey 'ranges for a quiltin' and give chitlin's and lye hominey. John comes and am inside when de patterrollers rides up to de door. Everybody gits quiet and John stands near de door, and when dey starts to come in he grabs de shovel full of hot ashes and thrown dem into de patterrollers faces. He gits through and runs off, hollerin' "Bird in de air!"[30]

115. As mentioned in the text, slave clothing was often so mended and patched that it almost resembled a quilt. This fine old photograph of a former slave shows him wearing a heavily patched suit of clothes. (Cook Collection, The Valentine Museum, Richmond, Virginia)

Children, to continue the metaphor, were more like stage props. They had no speaking parts—literally. Once a child was observed talking, he was usually sent home. Their role was limited to performing some minor service, such as untangling thread, retrieving something that had fallen to the floor, or bringing a requested item.

Children quickly learned to remain silently in the background, out of sight of the quilters, but not out of sound of the stories, gossip, and music.

A clue to what slaves wore to quilting parties can be found in the following reference from the article "Echoes from a Plantation Party," in an 1899 issue of *Southern Workman*: "Dress did not play a conspicuous part in the enjoyment of the party of the past. The dress of the field hands was exceedingly monotonous, the linsey-woolsey dress and the bed-ticking pantaloons being the chief styles."[31]

But the truth is that slaves did make an effort to individualize and "dress up" their shapeless, plain, and drab plantation garb with edging, trimming, and even patching. One ex-slave recalled mending articles of clothing so many times that the items began to resemble quilts: "De clothes den wusn't but ol' plain white cloth. Most of em' wus patched fum de legs to de waist. Some wus patched so till dey looked like a quilt."[32] Still another ex-slave commented on aspects of slave creativity, adding: "Make petticoat out of old dress en patch en patch till couldn' tell which place woave....Don get oak leaves an make a hat what to wear to church."[33]

The inventiveness and versatility with which slaves used materials is further evidenced by the following statement from another former slave:

Us have hats made out'n pine straw, long leaf pine straw, tied together in li'l bunches and platted round and round till it make a kinder hat. That pine straw great stuff in them days and us use it in lots of ways. Us kivered sweet 'taters with it to keep them from git freeze and hogs made beds ou'n it and folks too. Yes, sir, we slep on it.[34]

Individuality and creativity took other forms, too, as evidenced by the following:

Those who sewed could make the fabric in a style that suited them. Both Murat and Long referred to this happening. If fabric allotments were colorless or just alike for many other slaves, some slaves dyed the fabrics with vegetable dyes which were readily available. Some slaves knew how to embroider and knit and could use these techniques to decorate garments or make additional ones. When there was incentive for creativity, there was opportunity.[35]

Another area in which slaves could demonstrate creativity was hairstyles. Often elaborate hairstyles were worn to the more important quilting parties and other plantation festivities: "For days before the party the hair of the females was tightly wrapped with white strings to be unloosed on this momentous occasion, when it would show itself in the most beautiful waves."[36] African influence could also be seen here: "Twisted or plaited hair and the ubiquitous head cloth demonstrated this African influence, as did beads, earrings, and other jewelry."[37]

LINK TO SURVIVAL

Without doubt, slave-made quilts were products of a private world, so concealed that its very existence has long been denied. Not that the slaves quilted in secret; on the contrary, they sewed and knitted and quilted to provide for the entire plantation—the master's family as well as themselves. But in keeping with their condition of bondage, their craftsmanship has been ignored, even attributed to the plantation mistress whom they served.

Ironically, though slave quilting was perceived to be utilitarian, the slaves' careful stitches provided unique opportunities that even these African Americans did not fully recognize. Using techniques remembered from their West African origins, slaves passed on these skills, preserving their heritage for future generations. Unlike their ancestral tradition, however, women assumed the lead role in quilting. As they used their traditional techniques to quilt for master and slave alike, these African-American women found an outlet for their experiences and their emotions. Living under unending suspicion and uncertainty, they expressed their fears in the appliqués they cut, and the stitches they created, forging a link to survival even as they recalled their past.

Slave women channeled their despair into patterns of which they could be proud, in which they found fulfillment and a sense of self-worth. They also found support and camaraderie as they stitched. This bonding, rooted in the most desperate of human conditions—slavery—built a network among the quilters, and among their men and children who joined them on occasion. At times, this network included a plantation mistress who found a kinship in the quilting process.

Important as this sharing was for those slaves of more than a century past, its significance far exceeds the hours they stitched together. They could neither read nor write, yet in the quilts that survive, these slave women have left a powerful record—a hidden history, as it were—of their humiliation and tragedy, the milestones of their times and of their own lives.

It is a record to be read as it was written, not in words, but in feelings. Slave women cast long shadows, evidenced by their choice of fabrics, colors, and designs. These textiles clearly demonstrate the influence of the African-American experience in America and throughout the diaspora. They also remind us that the human mind, spirit, and talent can transcend the cruelest form of human degradation—slavery. Although slavery denied these women their physical freedom, it did not diminish their creative talent and artistic genius.

EPILOGUE

HARRIET POWERS: PORTRAIT OF AN AFRICAN-AMERICAN QUILTER*

Until recently very little was known about the life of Harriet Powers. Her name, her state of residence, and the existence of her two quilts, both in major museums, constituted her total legacy to the world. Yet it is precisely this powerful legacy that makes her worth knowing. Her quilts are visual masterpieces, jewels of creative imagination and artistic expression.

Harriet Powers was an African-American woman, originally a slave. Her entire communication with the world was visual and oral, which she expressed in narrative quilts using themes from her own experience and techniques from the age-old crafts of African Americans.

Fascinated with stories from oral tradition, Mrs. Powers used three types: local legends, biblical stories, and accounts of astronomical occurrences. Two local legends are included on her quilts: those of an independent hog named Betts, who ran from Georgia to Virginia (this is a traditional motif that became fastened to Georgia), and a man frozen at his jug of liquor. Each has the ring of a local incident, but is actually a traditional narrative known in several versions.

The core of her religious material dealt with legends about biblical heroes, usually those who had struggled successfully against overwhelming odds—Noah, Moses, Jonah, and Job. Some of her material can be considered "the Bible of the folk," in that she depicted traditional stories that extend biblical narratives. The serpent is portrayed in the Garden of Eden with feet, before he suffered God's curse. Adam's rib, from which Eve was made, is prominently featured. The miracle of creation itself provides the subject matter for several blocks.

In addition to biblical folk materials, Harriet Powers seemed especially interested in astronomical phenomena. Legendary accounts of actual events—eclipses, meteors, and comets—were infused with traditional motifs. As these legends circulated in oral tradition, they became formularized.

In Harriet Powers's quilt lies an almost intriguing classic tale of the South: the skilled work of the slave

*I originally wrote this article for the catalog *Missing Pieces: Georgia Folk Art 1770–1976*. Permission to reprint the article comes from the Georgia Council for the Arts.

116. Harriet Powers, who was born into slavery in 1837 and died in 1911. According to census data, she could neither read nor write. Her two known surviving quilts are owned by the Smithsonian Institution (fig. 117) and the Museum of Fine Arts, Boston (fig. 118). Note the sun motif that has been appliquéd to her apron. Scholars now feel that the sun motif is a religious symbol derived from the concept of circularity and the omniscience of God among the Bakongo of Africa. (Museum of Fine Arts, Boston, Massachusetts)

craftsman embedded in the creator's African heritage and preserved by the patron.

Although narrative quilts are distinctly an American art form, they use an appliqué technique traceable to historic Eastern and Middle Eastern civilizations, but having discernible roots in African culture. Harriet Powers's quilt forms a direct link to the tapestries traditionally made by the Fon people of Abomey, the ancient capital of Dahomey, West Africa.

Slaves brought to the South this knowledge of appliqué, a technique in which design elements are cut from cloth and sewn onto background fabric after first being narrowly turned under to form a hemmed edge. Men made the the appliqué in Dahomey, but the craft was part of the culture; in America, slave women perpetuated this kind of needlework.

Harriet Powers was born a slave in Georgia on October 29, 1837, during the period (1775–1875) when appliqué flourished in the South. The two quilts Mrs. Powers is known to have made follow the narrative tradition of depicting stories circulating orally, in different versions, and believed to be true, including biblical stories, and in her second quilt, local legends and astronomical phenomena.

Mrs. Powers's quilts can be compared with Dahomean tapestries in terms of design, construction technique, and the retention of stories associated with pictorial representations. The design process has been handed down for hundreds of years. Various figures are cut and appliquéd against a background cloth of black or gold. Humans are depicted in red or black. Animals are represented in colors not necessarily true to life, including purple, blue, green, and white. Patterns or templates of each design element are cut out of stiff paper and passed down from generation to generation in the Dahomean culture.

The construction technique may be derived from the bas-reliefs that decorated the wall of the palace in Abomey. Once cut, the cloth figures are basted onto the background cloth to ensure smoothness. Traditionally, the cloth is laid flat so that a running back or chain stitch can be directed away from the body to further ensure smoothness. In recent years, and such is the case with Mrs. Powers's quilts, the appliquéd cloth has been machine-made.

Often referred to as "living history books," these pictorial tapestries vary in subject from designer to designer. Tradition determines style and composition, but the individual designer decides which stories to relate, choosing from a common repertory. Stories from oral tradition and oral history are associated with each of the symbols. The Dahomeans most frequently reproduced symbols of the eleven kings who ruled Dahomey, connecting proverbs and sayings with the emblems of each king. Mrs. Powers's themes draw from well-known biblical stories, using symbols such as stars and figures of people and animals.

Just as biblical animals figure prominently in the stories illustrated by Harriet Powers, so many of the Dahomean tapestries contain animals as the central figures of proverbs or as symbols representing kings. Many of the kings are identified by totem animals, particularly the buffalo, pig, fish, bird, rooster, and lion. Stylistically, the animals on the Powers quilt and on the Dahomean tapestries are very similar. In both cases, the progression indicates the developing action through symbols.

Harriet Powers's fascination with biblical animals and characters probably stemmed from hearing vivid sermons in church on Sundays. According to Jennie Smith, the white woman who bought her first quilt, Mrs. Powers committed these sermons to memory and translated her impressions onto her quilts. Miss Smith observed that as evidence of her fondness for animals, Harriet expressed a desire to attend the Barnum and Bailey Circus when it came to Athens, Georgia, about 1890, because she wanted to see "all the Bible animals." But one compelling consideration that kept her away was the belief that it was a sin to go into a circus arena. (She may also have lacked the price of admission.) Her religion appeared to be fundamentalist, so that she believed in the literal word of the Bible.

Harriet Powers might have remained unknown outside of Athens had it not been for Jennie Smith, a Southern white woman of upper-middle-class connections. Miss Smith was responsible for bringing Mrs. Powers's first known quilt to the attention of the general public in Athens and Atlanta in the late nineteenth and early twentieth centuries.

Jennie Smith was born Oneita Virginia Smith in Athens in 1862. An artist of considerable local reputation, she received extensive training at the Lucy Cobb School in Athens and later in Baltimore, New York, and Paris. After living in the North and abroad, Jennie Smith returned to Athens and became head of the Art Department at Lucy Cobb for over fifty years. She was known affectionately by her many friends and pupils as "Miss Jennie." She died a spinster at the age of eighty-four in Athens in 1946.

Jennie Smith purchased Harriet Powers's first known quilt about 1890. Following her death, her estate was liquidated by Hal Heckman, head of the accounting department at the University of Georgia from 1921 to 1966. The quilt became part of the odds and ends of the estate that had not been specifically provided for in Miss Jennie's will. Mr. Heckman kept the quilt, eventually giving it to the Smithsonian, where it is now displayed.

Preserved along with the quilt was an eighteen-page handwritten narrative of about 1891, in which Miss Smith describes the series of events that led to her purchase of the 1886 quilt. The narrative is written in an extemporaneous prose style characteristic of the nineteenth century. She uses firm, vivid English, enlivened with humor and wit. She writes a little self-consciously, as if instinctively aware that her comments would be read by outsiders. Sprinkled throughout the narrative are references to pictorial symbols used by people in various cultures. These comments help to set Harriet Powers's quilt in its proper artistic and historic perspective.

This narrative is a major document because Jennie Smith is the only person to have left an eyewitness account of the remarkable Harriet Powers. It seems that Miss Smith viewed her as an exception within the general nineteenth-century idea of African-American inferiority. Although the narrative contains the stereotypical description of African Americans as musical but not artistic, religious but still liars and thieves, Miss Smith saw Harriet as a deeply religious woman of modesty and piety.

A Cotton Fair of 1886 first put the two women in touch with each other. The fair, according to Jennie Smith's narrative, had more attractions than the annual county fair; it included a Wild West show, two cotton weddings, and a circus.

Apparently the fair had a craft exhibit, where Jennie Smith saw Mrs. Powers's quilt hanging in a corner. Immediately fascinated by the originality of the design, she tracked down the maker. Miss Smith wrote: "I found the owner, a negro woman, who lived in the country on a little farm whereon she and her husband made a respectable living. She is about sixty-five years old, of a clear ginger cake color, and is a very clean and interesting woman who loves to talk of her 'old miss' and her life 'befo de wah.'" In fact, Harriet Powers was only forty-nine at the time of their first meeting. A life of hard work must have made her look considerably older.

Jennie Smith offered to buy the quilt after the 1886 fair, but Harriet refused to sell it then for any price. About 1890, Harriet, experiencing financial difficulty, sent word to Miss Smith that the quilt was now for sale. Jennie Smith was unable to purchase it in 1890, but apparently kept in contact with Mrs. Powers. In 1891 Jennie reopened negotiations. Her own words are very interesting:

> Last year I sent her word that I would buy it if she still wanted to dispose of it. She arrived one afternoon in front of my door in an ox-cart with the precious burden in her lap encased in a clean flour sack, which was still enveloped in a crocus sack.

> She offered it for ten dollars, but I told her I only had five to give. After going out consulting with her husband she returned and said "Owin to de hardness of de times, my ole man lows I'd better tech hit." Not being a new woman she obeyed.

> After giving me a full description of each scene with great earnestness, she departed but has been back several times to visit the darling offspring of her brain.

> She was only in a measure consoled for its loss when I promised to save her all my scraps.

It is one of the ironies of history that, heartbreaking as it was for Harriet to part with her quilt, its sale to Jennie Smith preserved it for posterity.

"It is my intention," wrote Jennie Smith, "to exhibit this quilt in the Colored Building at the Cotton States Exposition in Atlanta, and I hope all who are interested in art or religion in their primitive state will take the time to go to see it."

The 1895 Cotton States and International Exposition in Atlanta drew the participation of eleven Southern states, including Georgia, and several foreign countries. One of the outstanding features of this exhibition was a so-called Negro Building, constructed for ten thousand dollars from funds raised in the African-American community. Each participating state had an allocated exhibition area. The exhibits included products of various trades, such as carpentry, furniture making, brickwork, carriage and wagon building, wheelwrighting, harness making, and tinwork; agricultural products raised by African Americans on their own farms; mechanical goods assembled and built by African Americans, such as engines and boilers; photographs and models of African-American–owned businesses; paintings; and needlework.

Unfortunately, the official list of individual exhibitors no longer exists. It seems almost certain, however, that Jennie Smith did send the quilt to the Atlanta Exposition, where it was seen by the faculty ladies of Atlanta University. These women commissioned a second narrative quilt to be made by Harriet Powers as a gift in 1898 to the Reverend Charles Cuthbert Hall, president of the Union Theological Seminary and for many years chairman of the board of trustees of Atlanta University. Hall's son, the Reverend Basil Douglas Hall, inherited the quilt from his father and sold it to the Russian-American folk art collector Maxim Karolik, who gave it to the Museum of Fine Arts in Boston in 1964.

Though both her quilts have been preserved, little besides her birthdate is known about Harriet Powers. No information is available from orally transmitted family histories or reminiscences, because Mrs. Powers apparently has no known living descendants. Nor

117. Appliqué quilt by Harriet Powers that was discovered by Jennie Smith at a Cotton States Exposition in 1886. Harriet Powers eventually sold this quilt to Jennie Smith for $5.00 because she needed money, and she was only partially consoled by being allowed to visit "the offspring of her brain." (Smithsonian Institution, Washington, D.C.)

could dozens of elderly residents interviewed in Clarke and the surrounding counties in Georgia provide any clues about her life.

It is only from official records that we can glimpse bits and pieces of Harriet Powers's family history. Unfortunately, there are large gaps in the total picture because information about births, marriages, deaths, and wills was not recorded as completely for the African-American community as it was for whites in the nineteenth century. Valuable but limited information concerning the Powers family is contained in the census data, tax rolls, and records of deeds for Clarke County.

The census of 1870 for the state of Georgia firmly establishes the family in Clarke County, listing the names of Harriet Powers, her husband, and their three children. Armstead Powers, her husband and head of the household, was thirty-eight at the time the census was taken. Four years older than Harriet, he gave his occupation as farmhand. Harriet, thirty-four at the time, listed her occupation as "keeping house." The family owned no property in 1870, but estimated their personal estate to be worth three hundred dollars. Georgia was listed as the place of birth for the entire family. Census records indicate that neither Harriet nor Armstead could read or write. Two of the Powers

118. Appliqué Bible quilt by Harriet Powers, c. 1886, probably commissioned by faculty wives at Atlanta University. Fifteen panels depict biblical or verifiable astronomical events. (Museum of Fine Arts, Boston, Massachusetts)

children were apparently born in slavery: a daughter, Armanda, born in 1855, and a son, LeonJoe, born in 1860. Nancy, their youngest child, was born in 1866. All three children were living at home in 1870.

An examination of county tax records for a sixty-year period provides a few additional clues concerning the family's living circumstances. The name Armstead Powers, listed as "Arms," appeared for the first time in the 1870 Clarke County Tax Digest. In that year Powers paid one dollar in poll taxes, and no area of residence was indicated. The next entry appeared in 1873. Armstead Powers again paid one dollar in poll taxes. The family resided in that year in the Buck Branch, Winterville district of Clarke County. Records indicate that the family alternated between the Buck Branch

and Sandy Creek districts of Clarke County from 1870 to 1911. At least twelve years were spent in Buck Branch. The remaining twenty-four years, for which there are records, were spent in Sandy Creek.

The Powerses appeared to be a successful farm family. They gradually acquired a stock of animals, including horses, mules, cattle, and oxen. They owned plantation and mechanical tools. Their personal property, such as household furniture, clothing, and personal effects, increased yearly. And most important, the family managed to buy four acres of land, in two-acre allotments. Records in the Office of the Clerk of the County Court do not indicate exactly when the Powers family purchased the four acres of land that the Tax Digest indicated they owned. It can be presumed that this occurred sometime in the 1880s, since the census records do not indicate land ownership in the 1870s, and part of the land had been sold off by the early 1890s.

In spite of two decades of moderate prosperity, the family's fortunes had begun to decline by 1891. In that year Armstead Powers sold two acres of land to John R. Crawford of Clarke County for $177.[1] Three years later, in 1894, Armstead defaulted on his taxes. Harriet's and Armstead's names appeared jointly for the first time in the 1894 Tax Digest. Thereafter, only Harriet's name appeared on the annual tax rolls. Apparently Armstead left the family and the farm. He was definitely alive during this period, for he appeared at the Clarke County courthouse on February 13, 1901, to sell his remaining two acres of land for $359 to the same John R. Crawford who had purchased property from the couple in 1891.[2] It was a joint transaction. Both Harriet and Armstead Powers affixed their marks to the warranty deed. This transfer of property is the last official record of the Powers family.

From 1894 to 1910 Harriet maintained herself quite independently on farmland in Sandy Creek. She paid her yearly taxes, she borrowed money, and she mortgaged property.

As an example of her business acumen, in 1897 at the age of sixty, Harriet Powers decided to buy a buggy from a C. W. Cooper from Clarke County. A promissory note in the amount of $16.89 was drawn up in the Office of the Clerk of the County Court of Athens. Harriet agreed to pay the amount specified in a three-month period—August to November—with interest at the rate of 8 percent per year. The wording of the contract is interesting: "It is hereby agreed that the ownership of title to said buggy shall remain to said C. W. Cooper until this note is fully paid, and it is distinctly understood that I take all the risk of said dying."[3]

To ensure payment of the debt properly, Mrs. Powers mortgaged "one lot of land in Clarke County adjoining M. J. Kendricks on South side, joins McGuity of West and North and joins Armstead Powers on East, also M. J. Kendricks on East." On August 18, 1897, Harriet Powers made an x to indicate her signature to this agreement. Her name was written in by the county clerk.

It would appear that Mrs. Powers lived her remaining years alone. She did not remarry. Her children were grown when their parents separated. There is a strong possibility that they may have left Clarke County since their names do not appear on the tax rolls. Harriet may have maintained herself by sewing for people in the community. She either owned or had access to a sewing machine, as indicated by the machine stitching on her quilts.

Harriet Powers's standard of living became extremely low in her old age. Half of her household articles and farm animals were sold to meet expenses. Her total possessions—furnishings, farm tools, animals, and personal effects—amounted to eighty-two dollars in 1901, and only seventy dollars by 1911. In that year she died on a farm in Buck Branch. The word *dead* was penciled in beside her name in the 1911 Tax Digest. Her odyssey from Buck Branch to Sandy Creek to Buck Branch had come full circle. She was seventy-four years old.

The official records tell nothing, of course, of the contribution to American folk art for which Harriet Powers is remembered. With no idea of the value of her work, this woman who could neither read nor write nevertheless felt an obligation to record the meanings of the pictorial representations on her quilts. She dictated these to Jennie Smith, who contributed some amplifications; but the essential meaning and language are Harriet's own. The oral history behind four of the depictions has been identified. Explanations follow each depiction:

The dark day of May 19, 1780. The seven stars were seen 12.N. in the day. The cattle all went to bed, chickens to roost and the trumpet was blown. The sun went off to a small spot and then to darkness.

Dark days have been observed for centuries by meteorologists. As the atmosphere becomes polluted with smoke from forest fires, day is turned into night. In the period from 1706 to 1910, eighteen dark days were recorded. The most famous was May 19, 1780. Though popularly known as Black Friday, this day was characterized by an odor and gradually increasing yellowness. "During the dark day of 1780 ashes of burnt leaves, soot and cinders fell in some sections from forest fires in New York and Canada."[4] Scientists say this was confined to New England, but oral tradition concerning the dark day circulated throughout the country. Harriet Powers heard about it in Georgia. She was so deeply impressed by this spectacular occurrence, which had convinced observers that the end of the world was at hand, that she recorded it on her quilt.

Phineas Sprague of Melrose, Massachusetts, recorded in his diary an account of this extraordinary day:

Friday, May the 19th 1780.—This day was the most Remarkable day that ever my eyes beheld....About ten o'clock it began to Rain and grew vere dark and at 12 it was almost as dark as the Nite so that wee was obliged to lite our candels and Eate our dinner by candel lite at noon day. But between 1 and 2 o'clock it grew lite again but in the Evening the cloud caim over us again. The moon was about the full (but) it was the darkest nite that ever was seen by us in the world.[5]

Also:

Candles were lighted up in the houses; the birds having sung their evening songs, disappeared and became silent; the fowls retired to their roosts. The cocks were crowing all around as at break of day; objects could not be distinguished but at a very slight distance, and everything bore the gloom and appearance of night.[6]

John Greenleaf Whittier immortalized May 19, 1780, in a poem titled "Abraham Davenport." The poem concerns Colonel Davenport, a member of the governor's council in Connecticut, who objected to a motion to adjourn the council because of darkness and urged that candles be brought so that work could continue.

The falling of the stars on November 13, 1833. The people were frighten and thought that the end of time had come. God's hand staid the stars. The varmints rushed out of their beds.

Eyewitnesses to the extraordinary events of November 12-14, 1833, believed that "it was snowing fire," "the end of the world has come," "the sky is on fire," and "Judgement Day is here." What in fact took place was the famous Leonid meteor storm of 1833, which produced a dramatic display of shooting stars seen in greatest brilliance in North America. This meteor storm is significant because such events occur only three or four times a century, usually lasting no more than an hour. The Leonid storm of 1833, which was observed for eight hours, marks the beginning of scientific interest in meteors.

Scientific observers described the meteors as varying in size from the smallest visible points to fireballs equaling the moon in diameter. An unusual number of shooting stars was first seen as early as 10 P.M. on November 12. Their frequency increased until, between 2 and 6 A.M., it was impossible to calculate their number.[7] Estimates vary from 8,660 to 10,000 an hour. No sound whatever accompanied the display.

An eyewitness near Augusta, Georgia, gave the following account:

At about nine P.M. the shooting stars first arrested our attention, increasing in both number and brilliancy until 30 minutes past 2 A.M., when one of the most splendid sights perhaps that mortal eyes have ever beheld,

was opened to our astonished gaze. From the last mentioned hour until daylight the appearance of the heavens was awfully sublime. It would seem as if worlds upon worlds from the infinity of space were rushing like a whirlwind to our globe....[A]nd the stars descended like a snow fall to the earth....Occasionally one would dart forward leaving a brilliant train which...would remain visible, some of them for nearly fifteen minutes.[8]

As interesting as this event was in scientific circles, it is important to note that common people attached great significance to it. Eyewitness accounts were handed down, becoming the topic of comment and speculation for many generations. It became a time-fixing device by means of which important events, such as births and deaths, were determined by the general population, including former slaves.

At least a half-dozen scientific sources repeated the following account by a white planter in South Carolina:

I was suddenly awakened by the most distressing cries that ever fell on my ears. Shrieks of horror and cries of mercy I could hear from most of the negroes of the three plantations, amounting in all to about 600 to 800. While earnestly listening for the cause I heard a faint voice near the door, calling my name. I arose, and taking my sword, stood at the door. At this moment I heard the same voice still beseeching me to arise, and saying, "O my God, the world is on fire!" I then opened the door, and it is difficult to say which excited me the most—the awfulness of the scene, or the distressed cries of the negroes. Upwards of a hundred lay prostrate on the ground,—some speechless, and some with the bitterest cries, but with their hands raised, imploring God to save the world and them. The scene was truly awful; for never did rain fall much thicker than the meteors fell towards the earth; east, west, north, and south, it was the same.[9]

This account corroborates Harriet Powers's statement that "the people were frighten and thought that the end of time had come."

Cold Thursday, 10. of February, 1895. A woman frozen while at prayer. A woman frozen at a gateway. A man with a sack of meal frozen. Isicles formed from the breath of a mule. All blue birds killed. A man frozen at his jug of liquor.

According to *Climatological Data* for the state of Georgia (1895–98), the entire month of February 1895 was unseasonably cold, over six degrees below normal, with heavy snowfalls. On the morning of the eighth, the state experienced an unusually severe cold wave, which brought the temperature down to minus one degree in the Athens area. A second period of extreme cold, but not as severe, occurred several days later. In fact, February 10, which Mrs. Powers specifically mentioned, fell within the second cold snap. On that day the weather station in Athens registered the temperature as being twenty degrees in the early morning hours and thirty degrees at night. Sleet occurred at scattered points throughout the state. It should be noted that February 10, 1985, fell on a Sunday, rather than a Thursday.

Friday the eighth, then, was an extremely cold day for the southeastern United States, with a low temperature recorded at minus one degree. This two-day period, February 8–10, is probably the occasion of the frozen deaths suffered by humans and animals that Mrs. Powers recorded.

The red light night of 1846. A man tolling the bell to notify the people of the wonder. Women, children, and fowls frightened but Gods merciful hand caused no harm to them.

This information, though of considerable interest, is insufficient to determine the exact nature of the phenomenon. Fireballs or meteors are the only relevant occurrences recorded in scientific literature for the year 1846. *The American Journal of Science and Arts* (vol. 3, May 1847, pp. 125–26) states that meteoric showers were visible on the evenings of August 10 and 11, 1846. They could be seen from the northeast, southeast, southwest, and northwest. A cloudy sky and the presence of the moon hindered observations on the tenth, but a clear sky on the evening of the eleventh revealed twenty-three shooting stars from a southeasterly direction. Even more stars were visible from other directions.

Meteors falling thickly together, as they descended low in the air, appeared large and fiery, and the sky and air seemed to be in flames, even the earth appearing ready to take fire. It is this vision of August 10 and 11, 1846, that may have inspired Mrs. Powers's red light night.

Probably the real significance of Harriet Powers's explanations of her quilt blocks is that oral history turns out to be startlingly accurate. This former slave depicted stories that she had only heard, never read, and they paralleled scientific records. But times were changing in Harriet's day, and she knew intuitively that the quilts she had so carefully and lovingly created should be explained, in written form, for those who would examine them in later years. This she did, with the help of someone who could write. Thus she recorded those stories that had impressed her, just as in the quilt itself Harriet Powers expressed both her life experiences and her African heritage.

NOTES

The Slave Seamstress

1. George P. Rawick, ed., *Arkansas and Missouri Narratives*, vol. II of *The American Slave: A Composite Autobiography*. Contributions in Afro-American and African Studies II (1941; Westport: Greenwood, 1972), 313.

2. Mande Southwell Wahlman and Ellen King Terry, "Black American Folk Art: Quilts," *Craft International* (Spring 1982): 37.

3. James E. Newton, "Slave Artisans and Craftsmen: The Roots of Afro-American Art," James E. Newton and Ronald L. Lewis, eds., *The Other Slaves, Mechanics, Artisans, and Craftsmen* (Boston: G. K. Hall., 1978), 237.

4. Susan Walker, papers, Cincinnati Historical Society.

5. Rawick, *Arkansas Narratives*, vol. 8 of *American Slave*, 73.

6. Nathaniel Evans, and Family Collection, Plantation Record Books, Lousiana State University, Department of Archives, Baton Rouge, Lousiana.

7. Ulrich Bonnell Phillips, *American Negro Slavery: A Survey of the Supply, Employment and Control of Negro Labor as Determined by the Plantation Regime* (New York: D. Appleton, 1918), 267.

8. Margaret Thompson Ordonez, "A Frontier Reflected in Costume, Tallahassee, Leon County, Florida: 1824–1861" Ph.D. diss., Florida State University, 1977, 185-86.

9. Abigail Curlee, "A Study of Texas Slave Plantations, 1822–1865" Ph.D. diss., University of Texas at Austin, 1932, 55.

10. Rawick, *Arkansas Narratives*, vol. 10 of *American Slave*, 107.

11. Rawick, *Indiana and Ohio Narratives*, vol. 5 of *The American Slave*, Supplement Series 1. Contributions in Afro-American and African Studies 35 (Westport: Greenwood, 1977), 59.

12. Rawick, *Georgia Narratives*, vol. 12 of *American Slave*, 52.

13. Rawick, *Arkansas Narratives*, vol. 10 of *American Slave*, 289.

14. Rawick, *Georgia Narratives*, vol. 12 of *American Slave*, 117.

15. Rawick, *Arkansas Narratives*, vol. 10 of *American Slave*, 315–16.

16. Helen Mary Tinnin, "Helen Mary Kirkpatrick Tinnin, 1825–1893," in *Women in Early Texas*, ed. Evelyn M. Carrington (Austin: Jenkins, 1975), 259.

17. Raymond B. Pinchbeck, *The Virginia Negro Artisan and Tradesman* (Richmond: William Byrd, 1926), 12.

18. Leonard Price Stavisky, "The Negro Artisan in the South Atlantic States, 1800–1860" Ph.D. diss., Columbia University, 1958, 79.

19. Stavisky, 88.

20. Stavisky, 63.

21. *Maryland Prerogative Court, Vol. 6, Wills, Liber B. 1688–1700*, 17 Sept. 1697, 151, Museum of Early Southern Decorative Arts (Winston-Salem, North Carolina) research files.

22. Pinchbeck, 30.

23. Marie Tyler-McGraw and Gregg D. Kimball, *In Bondage and Freedom*, Catalogue, The Valentine Museum, Richmond, Virginia, 1988, 25.

24. Advertisement, *City Gazette and Daily Advertiser* (Charleston, South Carolina) 2 February 1801, 3-col. 1, Museum of Early Southern Decorative Arts (Winston-Salem, North Carolina) research files.

25. Eugene Genovese, *Roll, Jordan, Roll: The World Slaves Made* (New York: Pantheon Books, 1974), 551.

26. Sally Graham Durand, "The Dress of the Antebellum Field Slave in Lousiana and Mississippi from 1830–1860" M.A. thesis, Louisiana State University, 1977, 16-17.

27. Meta Grimball, Diary No. 975, ms, 5-6, Southern Historical Collection of the University of North Carolina Library, Chapel Hill.

28. Tinnin, 259.

29. Ordonez, 186.

30. Rawick, *Arkansas Narratives*, vol. 8 of *American Slave*, 74.

31. Rawick, *Florida Narratives*, vol. 17 of *American Slave*, 162.

32. Rawick, *Kansas, Kentucky, Maryland, Ohio, Virginia, and Tennessee Narratives*, vol. 16 of *American Slave*, 22.

33. Harriet Jacobs, *Encore*, 4.2 (June 23, 1975), 28-29. (A full account of the life of Harriet Jacobs, born a slave, can be found in *Incidents in the Life of a Slave Girl*, published in Boston in 1861. This *Encore* piece is an excerpt.)

34. Dorothy Sterling, *Black Foremothers: Three Lives*, (Old Westbury: Feminist Press, 1979), 9–10.

35. Paula Jones, "Slave Women in the Old South," M.A. thesis, Southern Methodist University, 1934, 44.

36. Sara Haynesworth, Gayle Diary, ms, Mon., Oct. 6, 1834, 177–78, W. Stanley Hoole, Special Collections Library, University of Alabama.

Quilting in the Quarters

1. Rawick, *Georgia Narratives*, vol. 13 of *American Slave*, 198.

2. Rawick, *Texas Narratives*, vol. 4 of *American Slave*, 108.

3. Rawick, *Unwritten History of Slavery*, vol. 18 of *American Slave*, 157.

4. Rawick, *Arkansas Narratives*, vol. 10 of *American Slave*, 45.

5. Rawick, *Mississippi Narratives*, vol. 6 of *American Slave*, suppl. ser. 1, 251.

6. Rawick, *Georgia Narratives*, vol. 12 of *American Slave*, 133.

7. Rawick, *Texas Narratives*, vol. 5 of *American Slave*, 196.

8. Rawick, *Oklahoma and Mississippi Narratives*, vol. 7 of *American Slave*, 103.

9. Rawick, *Georgia Narratives*, vol. 12 of *American Slave*, 87.

10. Rawick, *Kansas, Kentucky, Maryland, Ohio, Virginia, and Tennessee Narratives*, vol. 16 of *American Slave*, 63.

11. Rawick, *Georgia Narratives*, vol. 13 of *American Slave*, 74.

12. Rawick, *Alabama and Indiana Narratives*, vol. 6 of *American Slave*, 414.

13. Rawick, *Georgia Narratives*, vol. 12 of *American Slave*, 307.

14. Rawick, *Georgia Narratives*, vol. 3 of *American Slave*, suppl. ser. 1, 180.

15. Rawick, *Georgia Narratives*, vol. 13 of *American Slave*, 266.

16. Rawick, *Arkansas Narratives*, vol. 9 of *American Slave*, 280.

17. Rawick, *Alabama and Indiana Narratives*, vol. 6 of *American Slave*, 52.

18. Rawick, *Oklahoma and Mississippi Narratives*, vol. 7 of *American Slave*, 230.

19. Rawick, *Texas Narratives*, vol. 4 of *American Slave*, 177.

20. Rawick, *North Carolina Narratives*, vol. 15 of *American Slave*, 194–95.

21. Rawick, *Mississippi Narratives*, vol. 6 of *American Slave*, suppl. ser. 1, 248.

22. Rawick, *Mississippi Narratives*, vol. 6 of *American Slave*, suppl. ser. 1, 39.

23. Rawick, *Oklahoma and Mississippi Narratives*, vol. 7 of *American Slave*, 165–64.

24. Rawick, *Arkansas and Missouri Narratives*, vol. 11 of *American Slave*, 285–86.

25. Rawick, *Arkansas Narratives*, vol. 8 of *American Slave*, 72.

26. Rawick, *Georgia Narratives*, vol. 12 of *American Slave*, 240.

27. Rawick, *North Carolina and South Carolina Narratives*, vol. 11 of *American Slave*, suppl. ser. 1, 18.

28. Rawick, *Arkansas Narratives*, vol. 10 of *American Slave*, 59.

29. Rawick, *Texas Narratives*, vol. 4 of *American Slave*, 18.

30. Rawick, *North Carolina Narratives*, vol. 15 of *American Slave*, 63.

31. Ordonez, 185.

32. Genovese, 558.

33. William Bascom, *Shango in the New World* (Austin: African and Afro-American Research Institute, University of Texas Press, 1972), 10.

34. Rawick, *North Carolina Narratives*, vol. 15 of *American Slave*, 249.

35. Rawick, *Arkansas Narratives*, vol. 10 of *American Slave*, 109–10.

36. Rawick, *Mississippi Narratives*, vol. 6 of *American Slave*, suppl. ser. 1, 259.

37. Rawick, *South Carolina Narratives*, vol. 3 of *American Slave*, 180.

38. Rawick, *Florida Narratives*, vol. 17 of *American Slave*, 255.

39. Rawick, *Mississippi Narratives*, vol. 9 of *American Slave*, suppl. ser. 1, 1778.

40. Rawick, *Georgia Narratives*, vol. 13 of *American Slave*, 317.

41. Rawick, *Mississippi Narratives*, vol. 10 of *American Slave*, suppl. ser. 1, 2296.

42. Rawick, *Texas Narratives*, vol. 5 of *American Slave*, 74.

43. Rawick, *Kansas, Kentucky, Maryland, Ohio, Virginia, and Tennessee Narratives*, vol. 16 of *American Slave*, 29.

44. Rawick, *Alabama, Arizona, Arkansas, District of Columbia, Florida, Georgia, Indiana, Kansas, Maryland, Nebraska, New York, North Carolina, South Carolina, Oklahoma, Rhode Island, and Washington Narratives*, vol. 1 of *The American Slave*, Supplemental Series 2. Contributions in Afro-American and African Studies 49 (Westport: Greenwood, 1979), 347–48.

45. Rawick, *Texas Narratives*, vol. 4 of *American Slave*, 107.

46. Rawick, *North Carolina Narratives*, vol. 15 of *American Slave*, 129–30.

47. Rawick, *Texas Narratives*, vol. 5 of *American Slave*, 66.

48. Rawick, *Texas Narratives*, vol. 4 of *American Slave*, 55.

49. Emily P. Burke, *Reminiscences of Georgia*, (Oberlin: J. M. Fitch, 1850), 15.

50. Rawick, *Arkansas Narratives*, vol. 9 of *American Slave*, 85.

51. Rawick, *Unwritten History of Slavery*, vol. 18 of *American Slave*, 229.

52. Rawick, *Texas Narratives*, vol. 5 of *American Slave*, 120.

53. Rawick, *Florida Narratives*, vol. 17 of *American Slave*, 339.

54. Rawick, *Arkansas and Missouri Narratives*, vol. 11 of *American Slave*, 64.

55. Rawick, *Georgia Narratives*, vol. 12 of *American Slave*, 151.

56. Rawick, *Arkansas Narratives*, vol. 10 of *American Slave*, 128.

57. Rawick, *Arkansas Narratives*, vol. 8 of *American Slave*, 48.

58. Stavisky, 37.

59. "Miscellaneous Prose," WPA Folklore Collection (Accession no. 1574, Box 1), Special Collections, University of Virginia, Charlottesville.

60. Stavisky, 169.

61. Gloria L. Main, *Tobacco Colony: Life in Early Maryland, 1650–1720*, (Princeton: Princeton University Press, 1982), 137.

62. "Slave Speech," WPA Folklore Collection (Accession no. 1574, Box 2), Special Collections, University of Virginia, Charlottesville.

63. Rawick, *South Carolina Narratives*, vol. 3 of *American Slave*, 35.

64. Rawick, *Arkansas Narratives*, vol. 9 of *American Slave*, 182.

65. Rawick, *Georgia Narratives*, vol. 12 of *American Slave*, 284.

66. Rawick, *Arkansas and Missouri Narratives*, vol. 11 of *American Slave*, 237.

67. Rawick, *North Carolina Narratives*, vol. 15 of *American Slave*, 70.

68. Rawick, *Mississippi Narratives*, vol. 7 of *American Slave*, suppl. ser. 1, 616.

69. Genovese, 201.

The Quilting Party

1. Rawick, *Unwritten History of Slavery*, vol. 18 of *American Slave*, 24.

2. Rawick, *Kansas, Kentucky, Maryland, Ohio, Virginia, and Tennessee Narratives*, vol. 16 of *American Slave*, 62.

3. Rawick, *Georgia Narratives*, vol. 13 of *American Slave*, 283.

4. Rawick, *Georgia Narratives*, vol. 12 of *American Slave*, 217.

5. Rawick, *Georgia Narratives*, vol. 12 of *American Slave*, 348.

6. Rawick, *Florida Narratives*, vol. 17 of *American Slave*, 330.

7. Rawick, *Texas Narratives*, vol. 5 of *American Slave*, 136.

8. Thadeus Street Boinest, Diary (1821–1827), ts, 89, in library of Lutheran Seminary, Columbia, South Carolina.

9. Rawick, *Georgia Narratives*, vol. 12 of *American Slave*, 260.

10. Rawick, *Arkansas and Missouri Narratives*, vol. 11 of *American Slave*, 139–40.

11. Rawick, *Georgia Narratives*, vol. 12 of *American Slave*, 296.

12. Rawick, *Georgia Narratives*, vol. 12 of *American Slave*, 23–24.

13. Rawick, *South Carolina Narratives*, vol. 2 of *American Slave*, 175.

14. Rawick, *Unwritten History of Slavery*, vol. 18 of *American Slave*, 36–37.

15. Rawick, *Arkansas Narratives*, vol. 9 of *American Slave*, 291–92.

16. Rawick, *Unwritten History of Slavery*, vol. 18 of *American Slave*, 300.

17. Rawick, *Georgia Narratives*, vol. 13 of *American Slave*, 99–100.

18. Rawick, *Georgia Narratives*, vol. 12 of *American Slave*, 132.

19. Rawick, *Georgia Narratives*, vol. 13 of *American Slave*, 6.

20. Rawick, *North Carolina Narratives*, vol. 14 of *American Slave*, 191.

21. Rawick, *South Carolina Narratives*, vol. 3 of *American Slave*, 264.

22. Rawick, *Unwritten History of Slavery*, vol. 18 of *American Slave*, 146.

23. Rawick, *Oklahoma Narratives*, vol. 12 of *American Slave*, suppl. ser. 1, 66–67.

24. Rawick, *Arkansas Narratives*, vol. 10 of *American Slave*, 301.

25. Donald J. Waters, *Strange Ways and Sweet Dreams: Afro-American Folklore from the Hampton Institute*, (Boston: G. K. Hall, 1983), 49–50.

26. Rawick, *Georgia Narratives*, vol. 13 of *American Slave*, 63.

27. Rawick, *Georgia Narratives*, vol. 12 of *American Slave*, 228.

28. Rawick, *Arkansas Narratives*, vol. 9 of *American Slave*, 291.

29. Rawick, *Georgia Narratives*, vol. 12 of *American Slave*, 132.

30. Rawick, *Texas Narratives*, vol. 5 of *American Slave*, 248.

31. Daniel Webster Davis, "Echoes from a Plantation Party," *Southern Workman* 28.2 (Feb. 1899): 56.

32. Rawick, *Georgia Narratives*, vol. 12 of *American Slave*, 324.

33. Rawick, *South Carolina Narratives*, vol. 2 of *American Slave*, 190.

34. Rawick, *Texas Narratives*, vol. 5 of *American Slave*, 12.

35. Ordonez, 191.

36. Davis, 56.

37. Philip David Morgan, "The Development of Slave Culture in Eighteenth Century Plantation America" Ph.D. diss., University College, London, 1977, 383.

Epilogue

1. Deed Record K.K., Clarke County, Office of Clerk of County Court, Athens, Georgia, 1891.

2. Deed Record K.K., Clarke County, 1891.

3. Record of Mortgages Z, Clarke County, Georgia, Office of Clerk of County Court, Athens, Georgia, 1897.

4. Helen Sawyer Hogg, *Out of Old Books* (Toronto: David Dunlap Observatory, University of Toronto Press, 1974), 186–87.

5. Joseph Ashbrook, "Darkness at Noon," *Sky and Telescope* (Apr. 1964), 219.

6. Ashbrook, 219.

7. Daniel Kirkwood, *Comets and Meteors* (Philadelphia: J. B. Lippincott, 1873), 69.

8. Charles P. Oliver, *Meteors* (Baltimore: Williams and Wilkens, 1925), 25.

9. Mary Proctor, *The Romance of Comets* (New York: Harper and Brothers, 1926), 171.

BIBLIOGRAPHY

Periodicals

Adams, Marie Jeanne. "The Harriet Powers Pictorial Quilts." *Black Arts Magazine* 3.4 (Oct.-Dec. 1977): 12–28.

"Afro-American Tradition in Decorative Arts at the National Museum of History and Technology (D.C.)." *Black Heritage* 19.1 (Sept.-Oct. 1979): 11–18.

Agonito, Joseph. "St. Inigoes Manor: A Nineteenth Century Jesuit Plantation." *Maryland Historical Magazine* 72 (Spring 1977): 83–98.

Ashbrook, Joseph. "Darkness at Noon," *Sky and Telescope* (Apr. 1964): 219.

Astrachan, Anthony. "The Black Woman as Slave: Proud and Resourceful, Strong and Dignified, Courageous, Possesses a High Sense of Responsibility." *Encore* 4.2 (June 23, 1975): 34–35

Benberry, Cuesta. "Afro-American Women and Quilts." *Uncovering* (Mar. 1980): 2–10.

Bennett, Lerone, Jr. "No Crystal Stair: The Black Woman in History." *Ebony* 32.10 (Aug. 1971): 164–70.

_____. "The World of the Slave: The Making of Black America, part VII." *Ebony* 26.4 (Feb. 1971): 44–56.

Bertleth, Rosa Groce. "Jared Ellison Groce." *The Southwestern Historical Quarterly* 20.4 (Apr. 1917): 358–68.

Bradley, A. G. "Some Plantation Memories." *Blackwood's Edinburgh Magazine* 161 (Jan.-June 1987): 331–41.

Bradley, W. K. "Negroes in the Kentucky Mountains." *Crisis* 22.2 (June 1921): 69–71.

Brown, Minnie Miller. "Black Women in American Agriculture." *Agricultural History* 50 (Jan. 1976): 202–12.

Burnham, Dorothy. "The Life of the Afro-American Woman in Slavery." *International Journal of Women's Studies* 1 (July-Aug. 1978): 363–77.

Chase, Judith Wragg. "Ante-Bellum Black Craftsmen." *Southern Folklore Quarterly* 42 (1978): 152–57.

Condra, Nora Lee. Interview. *Quilter's Newsletter Magazine* (Jan. 1982): 32–33.

Davis, Angela. "Reflections on the Black Woman's Role in the Community of Slaves." *The Black Scholar* 3 (Dec. 1971): 2–18.

Davis, Daniel Webster. "Echoes from a Plantation Party." *Southern Workman* 28.2 (Feb. 1989): 54–59.

Dirks, Robert. "Slave's Holiday." *Natural History* 84 (Dec. 1975): 82–90.

Farrison, W. Edward. "Clotel, Thomas Jefferson, and Sally Hemings." *College Language Association Journal* 17 (Dec. 1973): 147–74.

Ferris, William R., Jr. "Black Delta Religion." *Mid-South Folklore* 2 (Spring 1974): 27–33.

"Folklore Scrap-book." *The Journal of American Folklore* 50 (Oct.-Dec. 1892): 328–32.

Gibson, George H. "The Mississippi Market for Woolen Goods: An 1822 Analysis." *Journal of Southern History* 31.1 (Feb. 1965): 80–90.

Glover, Flavin F. "An Alabama Quilt Collection." *Uncoverings* (May 1981): 8–14.

Goodson, Martia Graham. "The Slave Narrative Collection: A Tool for Reconstructing Afro-American Women's History." *Western Journal of Black Studies* 3 (Summer 1979): 116–22.

Griffin, Richard, and Diffee W. Standard. "The Cotton Textile Industry in Ante-Bellum North Carolina. Part 2: An Era of Boom and Consolidation, 1830–1860." *The North Carolina Historical Review* 34 (Apr. 1957): 131–64.

Jacobs, Harriet. "The Auction Block Ends a Dream." *Encore* 42 (June 23, 1975): 28–29.

Labinjoh, Justin. "The Sexual Life of the Oppressed: An Examination of the Family Life of Ante-Bellum Slaves." *Phylon: The Atlanta University Review of Race and Culture* 3 (1974): 375–97.

Ladner, Joyce A. "The Women: Conditions of Slavery Laid the Foundation for Their Liberation." *Encore* 30.10 (Aug. 1975): 76–81.

Lewis, Maggie. "Afro-American Quilts: Patching Together African Aesthetics, Colonial Craft." *Christian Science Monitor* Sec. B (Dec. 1, 1982): 6–9

Moore, Janie Gilliard. "Africanisms Among Blacks of the Sea Islands." *Journal of Black Studies* 10 (June 1980): 467–80.

Nelson, William. "The American Newspapers of the Eighteenth Century as Sources of History." *Annual Report of the American Historical Association* 1 (1908): 211–22.

Newman, Debra L. "Black Women in the Era of the American Revolution in Pennsylvania." *The Journal of Negro History* 61.3 (July 1976): 276–89.

Parkhurst, Jessie W. "The Role of the Black Mammy in the Plantation Household." *The Journal of Negro History* 23 (July 1938): 349-69.

Peek, Phil. "Afro-American Material Culture and the Afro-American Craftsman." *Southern Folklore Quarterly* 42 (1978): 109-34.

Perdue, Charles L., Jr. "Slave Life Styles in Early Virginia." *Proceedings of the Pioneer America Society* 11 (1973): 54-58.

Preyer, Morris W. "The Historian, the Slave, and the Ante-Bellum Textile Industry." *Journal of Negro History* 44.2 (April 1961): 68-82.

Quarterly Publication of the Historical and Philosophical Society of Ohio 6.2 and 6.3 (June and Sept. 1912). Comprises *Movement in Ohio to Deport the Negro* by Henry Noble Sherwood, and *Reprints of Two Pamphlets upon Colonization*. Cincinnati, Ohio: Jennings and Graham, 1912.

Reidy, Joseph P. "'Negro Election Day' and Black Community Life in New England, 1750-1860." *Marxist Perspectives* 1 (Fall 1978): 102-17.

Roediger, David. "The Meaning of Africa for the American Slave." *Journal of Ethnic Studies* 4 (Winter 1977): 1-15.

Schwartz, Jack. "Men's Clothing and the Negro." *Phylon: The Atlanta University Review of Race and Culture* 24 (Fall 1963): 224-31.

Schweninger, Loren. "A Slave Family in the Ante-Bellum South." *Journal of Negro History* 60 (Jan. 1975): 29-44.

Scott, Anne Firor. "Women in a Plantation Culture: Or What I Wish I Knew About Southern Women." *South Atlantic Urban Studies* 2 (1978): 24-33.

_____. "Women's Perspective on the Patriarchy in the 1850's." *Journal of American History* 61 (June 1974): 52-64.

Sides, Sudie Duncan. "Slave Weddings and Religion: Plantation Life in the Southern States before the American Civil War." *History Today* 24 (Feb. 1974): 77-87.

Smith, Eleanor. "Historical Relationships Between Black and White Women." *Western Journal of Black Studies* 4 (Winter 1980): 251-55.

Szwed, John F. "Africa Lies Just Off Georgia: Sea Islands Preserve Origins of Afro-American Culture." *Africa Report* 15 (Oct. 1970): 29-31.

Taylor, Orville W. "'Jumping the Broomstick': Slave Marriage and Morality in Arkansas." *The Arkansas Historical Quarterly* 17 (Autumn 1958): 217-31.

Tillman, Katherine Davis. "Afro-American Women and Their Work." *A.M.E. Church Review* (Apr. 1895): 477-99.

Tutwiler, Julia R. "Mammy." *The Atlantic Monthly* 91 (1903): 60-70.

Twining, Mary A. "African/Afro-American Artistic Community." *Journal of African Studies* 2 (Winter 1975-76): 569-78.

Uya, Okon Edet. "Life in the Slave Community." *Afro-American Studies* 1 (1971): 281-90.

Wahlman, Maude and Ellen King Terry. "Black American Folk Art: Quilts." *Craft International* (May 1982): 37-38.

Walker, Alice. "In Search of Our Mothers' Gardens: Honoring the Creativity of the Black Woman." *Jackson State Review* 6 (Summer 1974): 44-53.

Winslow David J. "A Negro Corn-shucking." *Journal of American Folklore* 86 (Jan.-March 1973): 61-62.

Books

Andrews, Granett. *Reminiscences of an Old Georgia Lawyer.* Atlanta: Franklin Steam Printing House, 1870.

Avirett, James Battle. *The Old Plantation: How We Lived in Great House and Cabin Before the War.* New York: F. Tennyson Neely, 1901.

Bascom, William. *Shango in the New World.* Austin: African and Afro-American Research Institute, University of Texas Press, 1972.

Bright, Alfred L., Sarah Brown Clark, Lawrence E. Amadi, Syretha Cooper, Clarence Barnes, and Daniel J. O'Neill. *An Interdisciplinary Introduction to Black Studies* (History, Sociology, Art and Philosophy of Black Civilization). Dubuque: Kendall/Hunt, 1977.

Brownlee, W. Elliott, and Mary M. Brownlee, eds. *Women in the American Economy: A Documentary History, 1675 to 1929.* New Haven: Yale University Press, 1976.

Burke, Emily P. *Reminiscences of Georgia.* Oberlin: J. M. Fitch, 1850.

Carr, Lois Green, and Lorena S. Walsh. "The Planter's Wife: The Experience of White Women in Seventeenth-Century Maryland." Cott and Pleck, 25-27.

Carrington, Evelyn M., ed. *Women in Early Texas.* Austin: Jenkins, 1975.

Carroll, Berenice A., ed. *Liberating Women's History: Theoretical and Critical Essays.* Urbana: University of Illinois Press, 1976.

Carter, Doris Dorcas. "Refusing to Relinquish the Struggle: The Social Role of the Black Woman in Louisiana History." Macdonald, Kemp, and Hass, 163-89.

Chase, Judith Wragg. *Afro-American Art and Craft.* New York: Van Nostrand Reinhold, 1971.

Child, L. Maria, ed. *Incidents in the Life of a Slave Girl: Written by Herself (Linda Brent).* Boston: privately printed, 1861.

Cott, Nancy F., and Elizabeth H. Pleck, eds. *A Heritage of Her Own: Toward a New Social History of American Women*. New York: Simon and Schuster, 1979.

Delaney, Lucy, A. *From the Darkness Cometh the Light, or Struggles for Freedom*. St. Louis: J. T. Smith, [c. 1890].

DePauw, Linda Grant. *Founding Mothers: Women in America in the Revolutionary Era*. Boston: Houghton Mifflin, 1975.

Deutrich, Mabel E. and Virginia C. Purdy, eds. *Clio Was a Woman: Studies in the History of American Women*. Washington, D.C.: Howard University Press, 1980.

Dover, Cedric. "The Manual Arts." Newton and Lewis, 221–25.

Dubois, W. E. B. "The African Artist." Newton and Lewis, 171–74.

Elkins, Stanley M. "The Social Consequences of Slavery." Huggins, Kilson, and Fox, 1:138–53.

Emerson, William C. *Stories and Spirituals of the Negro Slave*. Boston: R.G. Badger; Gorham, 1930.

Escott, Paul D. *Slavery Remembered: A Record of Twentieth Century Slave Narratives*. Chapel Hill: University of North Carolina Press, 1979.

Ferrero, Pat, Elaine Hedges, and Julie Silver. *Hearts and Hands*. San Francisco: Quilt Digest, 1987.

Fox-Genovese, Elizabeth. *Within the Plantation Household: Black and White Women of the Old South*. Chapel Hill: University of North Carolina Press, 1988.

Frazier, E. Franklin. "Granny: The Guardian of the Generations." Watkins and David, 202–14.

Genovese, Eugene D. "Life in the Big House." Cott and Pleck, 290–97.

———. *Roll, Jordan, Roll: The World the Slaves Made*. New York: Pantheon Books, 1974.

Gordon, Linda, et al. "Historical Phallacies: Sexism in American Historical Writing." Carroll, 55–74.

Gray, Lewis Cecil. *History of Agriculture in the Southern United States to 1860*. Gloucester: Peter Smith, 1958.

Gregory, Chester W. "Black Women in Pre-Federal America." Deutrich and Purdy, 53–70.

Harley, Sharon. "Northern Black Female Workers: Jacksonian Era." Harley and Terborg-Penn, 5–16.

———, and Rosalyn Terborg-Penn. *The Afro-American Woman: Struggles and Images*. Port Washington: National University Publications-Kennikat, 1978.

Harris, Joel Chandler. "The Women of the South." *Southern Historical Society Papers*. Vol. 18. Ed. R. R. Brock. New York: Kraus Reprint, 1977, 277–81.

Hernton, Calvin C. "The Negro Woman." Watkins and David, 31–37.

Hogg, Helen Sawyer. *Out of Old Books*. Toronto: David Dunlap Observatory, University of Toronto Press, 1974.

Horton, Roberta. *Calico and Beyond: The Use of Patterned Fabric and Quilts*. Lafayette: C & T Publishing, 1986.

Huggins, Nathan I. "Afro-American History: Myths, Heroes, Reality." Huggins, Kilson, and Fox, 1:5–19.

———, Martin Kilson, and Daniel M. Fox, eds. *Key Issues in the Afro-American Experience*, 2 vols. New York: Harcourt, Brace, Jovanovich, 1971.

Hymnowitz, Carol, and Michaele Weissman. *A History of Women in America*. New York: Bantam, 1978.

Irvin, Helen Deiss. "Slave State." *Women in Kentucky*. Lexington: University Press of Kentucky, 1979, 48–66.

Jackson, Lela. "Rachel Whitfield (1814–1908)." Carrington, 289–93.

Jefferson, Thomas. *Thomas Jefferson's Farm Book, with Commentary and Relevant Extracts from Other Writings*, ed. Edwin Morris Betts. Charlottesville: University Press of Virginia, 1976.

Jensen, Joan M. *Loosening the Bonds: Mid-Atlantic Farm Women, 1750–1850*. New Haven: Yale University Press, 1986.

Jordan, Winthrop D. *White Over Black: American Attitudes Toward the Negro, 1550–1812*. Chapel Hill: University of North Carolina Press, 1968.

Kearney, Beele. *A Slaveholder's Daughter*. 7th ed. New York: Abbey, 1900.

Keckley, Elizabeth. *Behind the Scenes*. New York: G.W. Carleton, 1868.

Kirkwood, Daniel. *Comets and Meteors*, Philadelphia: J. B. Lippincott, 1873.

Lerner, Gerda. *Black Women in White America: A Documentary History*. New York: Pantheon, 1972.

———. "New Approaches to the Study of Women in American History." Carroll, 349–56.

Litwack, Leon F. *Been in the Storm So Long: The Aftermath of Slavery*. New York: Alfred A. Knopf, 1981.

Locke, Alain. "The Negro as Artist." Newton and Lewis, 205–207.

MacDonald, Anne L. *No Idle Hands: The Social History of American Knitting*. New York: Ballantine Books, 1988.

MacDonald, Robert R., John R. Kemp, and Edward F. Hass, eds. *Louisiana's Black Heritage*. New Orleans: Louisiana State Museum, 1979.

Magdol, Edward. *A Right to the Land: Essays on the Freedmen's Community*. Westport: Greenwood, 1977.

Main, Gloria L. *Tobacco Colony: Life in Early Maryland, 1650–1720*. Princeton: Princeton University Press, 1982.

McMorris, Penny. "Afro-American Quilts." *Quilting II.* Bowling Green: WBGU-TV, Bowling Green University Press, 1982, 53–57.

Newton, James E. "Slave Artisans and Craftsmen: The Roots of Afro-American Art." Newton and Lewis, 233–41.

_____, and Ronald L. Lewis, eds. *The Other Slaves: Mechanics, Artisans and Craftsmen.* Boston: G. K. Hall, 1978.

Oliver, Charles P. *Meteors.* Baltimore: Williams and Wilkens, 1925.

Owens, Leslie Howard. *This Species of Prosperity: Slave Life and Culture in the Old South.* New York: Oxford University Press, 1976.

Phillips, Ulrich Bonnell. *American Negro Slavery: A Survey of the Supply, Employment and Control of Negro Labor as Determined by the Plantation Regime.* New York: D. Appleton, 1918.

Piersen, William D. *Black Yankee: The Development of an Afro-American Subculture in Eighteenth-Century New England.* Amherst: University of Massachusetts Press, 1988.

Pinchbeck, Raymond B. *The Virginia Negro Artisan and Tradesman.* Richmond: William Byrd, 1926.

Porter, James A. "Negro Craftsmen and Artists of Pre-Civil War Days." Newton and Lewis. 209–20.

Procter, Mary. *The Romance of Comets.* New York: Harper and Brothers, 1926.

Ramsey, Bets, and Merikay Waldrogel. *The Quilts of Tennessee,* Nashville: Rutledge Hill, 1986.

Rawick, George P., ed. *The American Slave: A Composite Autobiography.* 19 vols. Contributions in Afro-American and African Studies 11. 1941. Westport: Greenwood, 1972.

_____. *The American Slave: A Composite Autobiography.* Supplement, series 1. 12 vols. Contributions in Afro-American and African Studies 35. Westport: Greenwood, 1977.

_____. *The American Slave: A Composite Autobiography.* Supplement, series 2. 10 vols. Contributions in Afro-American and African Studies 49. Westport: Greenwood, 1977.

_____. "West African Culture and North American Slavery: A Study of Culture Change among American Slaves in the Ante-Bellum South with Focus upon Slave Religion." *Migration and Anthropology: Proceedings of the 1970 Annual Spring Meeting of the American Ethnological Society.* Ed. Robert F. Spencer. Seattle: American Ethnological Society. University of Washington Press, 1970, 149–64.

Rowan, Richard L. *The Negro in the Textile Industry.* The Racial Policies of American Industry, Report No. 20. Philadelphia: University of Pennsylvania Press, 1970.

Ryan, Mary P. *Womanhood in America: From Colonial Times to the Present.* New York: Franklin Watts, 1983.

Smith, Barbara Clark. *After the Revolution: The Smithsonian History of Everyday Life in the Eighteenth Century.* New York: Pantheon Books, 1985.

_____. "The Female World of Love and Ritual: Relations Between Women in Nineteenth-Century America." Cott and Pleck, 311–42.

Spruill, Julia Cherry. *Women's Life and Work in the Southern Colonies.* New York: W. W. Norton, 1972.

Stampp, Kenneth M. "The Daily Life of the Southern Slave." Huggins, Kilson, and Fox, 1:116–37.

Staples, Robert. *The Black Woman in America: Sex, Marriage, and the Family.* Chicago: Nelson Hall, 1973.

Starobin, Robert S. *Industrial Slavery in the Old South.* New York: Oxford University Press, 1970.

Stavisky, Leonard P. "Negro Craftsmanship in Early America." Newton and Lewis, 193–203.

_____. "The Origins of Negro Craftsmanship in Colonial America." Newton and Lewis, 183–91.

Sterling, Dorothy. *Black Foremothers: Three Lives.* Old Westbury: Feminist Press, 1979.

Stuckey, Sterling. *Slave Culture: Nationalist Theory and the Foundations of Black America.* New York: Oxford University Press, 1987.

Tate, Thad W. *The Negro in Eighteenth-Century Williamsburg.* Charlottesville: University of Virginia Press, 1965.

Taylor, Joe Gray. "A New Look at Slavery in Louisiana." MacDonald, Kemp, and Hass, 190–208.

Terborg-Penn, Rosalyn. "Black Male Perspectives on the Nineteenth Century Woman." Harley and Terborg-Penn, 28–42.

Thompson, Robert F. *The Trans-Atlantic Tradition.* New York: Random House, 1980.

Tinnin, Helen Mary. "Helen Mary Kirkpatrick Tinnin, (1825–1893)." Carrington, 258–62.

Wahlman, Maude, and John Scully. "Aesthetic Principles in Afro-American Quilts." *Afro-American Folk Art and Crafts.* Ed. Williams R. Ferris, Jr. New York: Alfred A. Knopf, 1982.

Waters, Donald J. *Strange Ways and Sweet Dreams: Afro-American Folklore from the Hampton Institute.* Boston: G. K. Hall, 1983, 49–50.

Watkins, Mel, and Jay David, eds. *To Be a Black Woman: Portraits in Fact and Fiction.* New York: William Morrow, 1970.

Webber, Thomas L. *Deep Like the Rivers: Education in the Slave Quarter Community, 1831–1865.* New York: W. W. Norton, 1978.

Wetheimer, Barbara Mayer. *We Were There: The Story of Working Women in America*. New York: Pantheon Books, 1977.

Wiley, Bell Irvin. *Southern Negroes, 1861-65*. New Haven: Yale University Press, 1965.

Williams, Jean Lockwood. "Elizabeth Thomas Davis Bagley (1826-1911)." Carrington, 31-36.

Wilson, Miriam Bellangee. *Slave Days*. Charleston: Old Slave Mart Museum, 1956.

Museum Catalogues

Clarke, Rickle. "Shooting Stars." *Quilts and Carousels: Folk Art in Firelands*. Oberlin: Firelands Association for the Visual Arts, April 1983.

Freeman, Roland. *Something to Keep You Warm*. Jackson: Mississippi State Historical Museum, 1981.

Fry, Gladys-Marie. *Broken Star: Post-Civil War Quilts Made by Black Women*. Dallas: Museum of African-American Life and Culture, 1986.

_____. "Harriet Powers: Portrait of a Black Quilter." *Missing Places: Georgia Folk Art 1770-1976*. Atlanta: Atlanta Historical Society, 1976.

"Made by Hand." *Mississippi Folk Arts*. Jackson: Mississippi State Historical Museum, 1980.

McGraw, Marie Tyler and Gregg D. Kimball. *In Bondage and Freedom*. Richmond: The Valentine Museum, 1988.

Perry, Reginia. "Harriet Powers, 1837-1910." *Selections of 19th Century Afro-American Art*. New York: The Metropolitan Museum of Art, 1976.

_____. "Quilt Making." *Black Folk Art in America, 1930-1980*. Washington, D.C.: Corcoran Gallery of Art, 1982.

Stitches in Time: A Legacy of Ozark Quilts. Rodgers: Rodgers Historical Museum, 1986.

Vlach, John M. "Quilting." *The Afro-American Tradition in Decorative Arts*. Cleveland: Cleveland Museum of Art, 1978.

Wahlman, Maude, and Nan Becker. *Black Quilters*. New Haven: Yale School of Art, 1979.

Unpublished Sources (Theses, Dissertations, Private papers, Diaries, Museum files)

Advertisement. *City Gazette and Daily Advertiser* (Charleston, South Carolina) 2 February, 1801, 3-col. 1. Museum of Early Southern Decorative Arts research files.

Blackburn, Regina Lynn. "Conscious Agents of Time and Self: The Lives and Styles of African-American Women as Seen through Their Autobiographical Writings." Ph.D. diss., University of New Mexico, 1978.

Bogger, Tommy L. "The Slave and Free Black Community in Norfolk, 1775-1865." Ph.D. diss., University of Virginia, 1976.

Boinest, Thaddeus Street. Diary (1821-1827). Library of Lutheran Seminary in Columbia, South Carolina.

Corbett, Melville Fort. "A Preliminary Study of the Planter Aristocracy as a Folk Level of Life in the Old South." M.A. thesis, University of North Carolina, 1941.

Curlee, Abigail. "A Study of Texas Slave Plantations, 1822-1865." Ph.D. diss., University of Texas at Austin, 1932.

Deed Record K.K. Clarke County, Georgia. Office of the County Clerk, Athens, Georgia, 1891.

Durand, Sally Graham. "The Dress of the Ante-bellum Field Slave in Louisiana and Mississippi from 1830 to 1860." M. A. thesis, Louisiana State University, 1977.

Evans, Nathaniel and Family, Collection. Plantation Record Books. Louisiana State University, Department of Archives, Baton Rouge, Louisiana.

Grimball, Meta. Diary 975. Southern Historical Collection. University of North Carolina Library, Chapel Hill.

Hawkes, Alta Marcellus. "Food, Clothing and Shelter of the American Slave." Ph.D. diss., Southern Methodist University, 1936.

Haynesworth, Sarah. Gayle Diary, W. Stanley Hoole, Special Collections Library, University of Alabama.

Huber, Jo Anne Sellers. "Southern Women and the Institution of Slavery." M.A. thesis, Lomar University, 1980.

Jones, Bobby Frank. "A Cultural Middle Passage: Slave Marriage and Family in the Ante-Bellum South." Ph.D. diss., University of North Carolina at Chapel Hill, 1965.

Jones, Paula. "Slave Women in the Old South." M.A. thesis, Southern Methodist University, 1934.

Maryland Prerogative Court, Vol. 6, Wills, Liber B. 1688-1700, 151, 17 Sept. 1697. Museum of Early Southern Decorative Arts research files.

Mickel, Robina. "Some Customs and Superstitions of the Southern Negro." M.A. thesis, Columbia University, 1916.

"Miscellaneous Speech." Folder. Special Collections, Manuscript Department, University of Virginia, Charlottesville.

Morgan, Philip David. The Development of Slave Culture in Eighteenth Century Plantation America." Ph.D. diss., University College, London, 1977.

O'Brien, Mary Lawrence. "Slavery in Louisville During the Ante-Bellum Period: 1820-1860. A study of the effects of urbanization on the institution of slavery as it existed in Louisville, Kentucky." M.A. thesis, University of Kentucky, 1979.

Ordonez, Margaret Thompson. "A Frontier Reflected in Costume Tallahassee, Leon County, Florida: 1824-1861." Ph.D. diss., Florida State University, 1977.

Piersen, William D. "Afro-American Culture in Eighteenth Century New England: A Comparative Examination." Ph.D. diss. Indiana University, 1975.

Record of Mortgage Z. Clarke County, Georgia. Office of Clerk of County Court, Athens, Georgia, 1897.

"Slave Speech." Folder. Special Collections, Manuscript Department, University of Virginia, Charlottesville.

Stavisky, Leonard P. "The Negro Artisan in the South Atlantic States, 1800–1860: A Study of Status and Economic Opportunity with Special Reference to Charleston." Ph.D. diss., Columbia University, 1958.

Twining, Mary A. "An Examination of African Retentions in the Folk Culture of the South Carolina and Georgia Sea Islands." Ph.D. diss., Indiana University, 1977.

Wade, Melvin. "Through the Rabbit's Eye: Critical Perspectives on African-American Folk Culture of the Nineteenth Century." Unpublished manuscript, University of Texas at Austin, 1977.

Wahlman, Maude, "The Art of Afro-American Quilt Making: Origin, Development, and Significance." Ph.D. diss., Yale University, 1980.

Walker, Susan. Papers. Cincinnati Historical Society.

Weldon, Fred Olen, Jr. "Negro Folk Heroes." M.A. thesis, University of Texas, 1958

Winfield, Arthur Anison, Jr. "Slave Holidays and Festivities in the United States." Ph.D. diss., Atlanta University, 1941.

Wyatt, Emma Ollie. "Negro Folklore from Alabama." M.A. thesis, State University of Iowa, 1943.